MYSTERIES OF THE AFTERLIFE

RON JONES

HARVEST HOUSE PUBLISHERS
EUGENE, OREGON

Italicized emphasis in Scripture quotations is added by the author.

Cover by Writely Designed, Buckley, Washington

MYSTERIES OF THE AFTERLIFE

Published by Harvest House Publishers
Eugene, Oregon 97402
www.harvesthousepublishers.com

Library of Congress Cataloging-in-Publication Data
Jones, Ron, 1963-
Mysteries of the afterlife / Ron Jones.
pages cm
ISBN 978-0-7369-6400-5 (pbk.)
ISBN 978-0-7369-6401-2 (eBook)
1. Future life—Christianity. I. Title.
BT903.J66 2016
236'.2—dc23

2015021169

Printed in the United States of America

15 16 17 18 19 20 21 22 23 24 / VP-SK / 10 9 8 7 6 5 4 3 2 1

To Mom, who believed her son would one day write a book about Jesus. Rest in the peaceful presence of your Savior.
And to Dad, who always says he's proud of me.
I pray this answers your questions about the afterlife.

Acknowledgments

The writing of any book is possible but not inevitable. That's because no author writes alone. It takes a team of people to support the project and turn it into reality. I'm glad to welcome my new friends at Harvest House Publishers to my extended ministry team. I also feel blessed to be included on their list of esteemed authors. Many thanks go out to Bob Hawkins Jr., LaRae Weikert, and Terry Glaspey for meeting with me in New York City and Nashville to discuss my writing aspirations. Of course those meetings would never have taken place without the help of Mick and Julie Tingstrom, who provide the Joneses with constant laughter, inspiration, vision, and friendship for life! God used Julie to change the scope and trajectory of my ministry and fulfill a lifelong dream when she humbly said, "I'd like to introduce you to some of my friends."

Nick Harrison is also part of the Harvest House team and someone every author needs in his life. He is a kind, capable, gentle, and encouraging editor. Like the quarterback on a football team, an author drives the project down the field and gets it in the literary red zone; someone like Nick puts the book in the end zone by smoothing over the rough places and making the right editorial calls. I'm also grateful for the editorial input my friend Deane Allen gave me on the chapter titled "Eternity for Those Who Can't Believe," and for his and Linda's permission to include their story about baby Jacob.

God also blessed me with a beautiful wife and us with two extraordinary children. Team Jones fills my life with love, laughter, inspiration, and hope that tomorrow will always be a better day. My wife Cathryn deserves sainthood for enduring the ups and downs of life while married to a dreamer, a visionary pastor, and now an author who fastidiously pores over the right words, phrases, and sentences. Neither of us knew quite what we were getting ourselves into when we started this journey more than two decades ago. To my best friend and lover, thanks for still believing that God is faithful and full of grace, and that the best is yet to come! I love you and the way the Fab 4 does family life and ministry together.

Finally, thank you to my church family who first listened to their pastor deliver a series of messages on the afterlife and then provided feedback, to our Something Good Radio listening family who responded to the broadcast of that series with great interest and enthusiasm, to the Something Good Radio Board of Trustees for your constant prayers, encouragement, and wise counsel, and to my media agent Jack Hibbard and his wife Erin for your authentic friendship in Christ, prayer support, and advisement. It's no mystery why your collective love for and commitment to the Word of God still inspires me every day.

Ron Jones
Virginia Beach, Virginia

Contents

Introduction 9

1. A Traveler's Guide to Your Final Destination 13
2. Can We Really Live Forever? 19
3. Eternity in Our Hearts 23
4. The Last Enemy 29
5. Your Appointment with Death 35
6. Between Death and the Future Resurrection 41
7. Sixty Seconds After We Die 47
8. Can We Communicate with the Dead? 57
9. Saul and the Witch of Endor 63
10. Are You a Citizen of Heaven? 69
11. Is Your Name Written in Heaven? 77
12. The Father's Big House 85
13. Is Heaven for Real? 95
14. Heaven and the New Jerusalem 101
15. Imagine There's a Heaven 109
16. Will the Dead Rise Again? 121
17. The Seven Resurrections of the Dead 131
18. Can God Resurrect a Cremated Body? 139
19. Was John Lennon Right About Hell? 149
20. What Jesus Said About Hell 159
21. The Believer's Day of Reward 169
22. Angels Watching Over Us 179
23. Angels in the Realms of Glory and Beyond 189
24. Eternity for Those Who Can't Believe 197

An Afterword About the Afterlife 207

Notes 213

About the Author 217

Introduction

Do you love a good mystery?

Suspense, enigmatic characters, and puzzling plot lines keep readers turning the page of a good mystery novel.

Real-life mysteries interest us too. Like whatever happened to Jimmy Hoffa? What about the fate of Amelia Earhart? What is Stonehenge all about? Area 51? Do UFOs exist? What's up with the Bermuda Triangle? Is Bigfoot just a myth? What significance does the Shroud of Turin hold?

All these mysteries and more arouse our curiosity precisely because they *are* mysteries.

For many people, the afterlife is fraught with mystery. I assume because you're reading this book, that's true of you. You, like most of us, possess a curiosity about life after death. Does it exist, and if it does, what can we expect the moment our heart stops beating?

Are heaven and hell real places or old concepts hanging over from a less-enlightened era? Are we reincarnated? Or is the grave the end of it all and there is no such thing as an afterlife? There's no shortage of speculation about the afterlife for the same reason there's no shortage of interest in the subject. Books have been written about it, sermons preached about it, movies filmed about it. All this, even though the subject of death still makes us uncomfortable and discussing it remains taboo. Want to empty a room? Just start a conversation about death.

The fact remains death is a mystery. We often hear the phrase "God works in mysterious ways." While that's true, those words do not appear anywhere in the Bible. They belong with other chapter-and-verse myths like "God helps those who help themselves" and "Cleanliness is next to godliness." The Bible *does* say, "The secret things belong to the LORD our God, but the things that are revealed belong to us and to our children forever, that we may do all the words of this law" (Deuteronomy 29:29).

God is a revealer of secrets and mysteries. He has revealed the mystery of life, eternity, and Himself through creation, in our conscience, within the words of Scripture, and through His Son Jesus Christ. God's revelation *always* trumps human speculation, which is why any conjecture about eternal things based on human reason and personal experience is suspect. However, what God has revealed "belongs to us and to our children forever." This includes the amazing secrets of the afterlife.

In the Bible, a "mystery" is something that was once concealed but is now revealed. God alone chooses what to reveal and what to conceal until a later time. The word "mystery" appears thirty times in the pages of holy writ, especially in the inspired writings of the apostle Paul, which are found in the New Testament. For example, he mentions:

- The mystery of godliness (1 Timothy 3:16)
- The mystery of Israel's salvation (Romans 11:25)
- The mystery of Christ's Second Coming (1 Corinthians 15:51)
- The mystery of the gospel (Ephesians 3:6; 6:19)
- The mystery of Christ (Ephesians 3:4; Colossians 4:3)
- The mystery of the church (Ephesians 5:32)
- The mystery of God's will (Ephesians 1:9)
- The mystery of marriage (Ephesians 5:31-32)
- The mystery of lawlessness (2 Thessalonians 2:7)

Of course, nothing is more mysterious to us than what happens moments after we die. Death eventually touches us all. For this reason we're curious, and for this reason God has chosen to reveal aspects of the afterlife that are vital for us to know.

The book you're holding in your hands, *Mysteries of the Afterlife: Exploring Its Amazing Secrets,* attempts to answer those questions and give us a glimpse of these vital aspects.

May God bless you and comfort you as you read.

When the perishable puts on the imperishable, and
the mortal puts on immortality,
then shall come to pass the saying that is written:
"Death is swallowed up in victory."
"O death, where is your victory?
O death, where is your sting?"

(1 Corinthians 15:54-55)

1

A Traveler's Guide to Your Final Destination

As a pastor for more than twenty years, I've conducted my fair share of funerals. In a weird kind of way, it's one of my more enjoyable pastoral duties. That might sound strange, but because funerals are for the living not the dead, they provide a rare opportunity to get real with people, remind them of their own mortality, and speak pointedly about eternal things. It's a moment made for the gospel to shine.

One of the most complicated funerals I ever conducted was for a man I never met. His wife and children attended the church I pastored, but I never saw him. One day he died in a freak accident when his private airplane collided with another one in midair. The accident happened above a major freeway in Houston and made the evening news. Of course the man's wife and kids were devastated. But her devastation quickly turned to anger when she learned he owned an airplane she knew nothing about. That was only the beginning of her discovery.

For years, the husband convinced his wife they were struggling financially. They lived in a modest home and money was always in short supply. She did the best she could to clothe the kids for school and prepare well-balanced meals for them. But when he died, she learned he had been living a double life and shortchanging his own family. He actually did quite well in a business he kept from his wife's knowledge. He gave her enough money to run the modest household but used the rest to collect an array of toys, including airplanes, boats, motorcycles, condos, and more. In a twist of irony, everything now all belonged to her.

I was asked to conduct the funeral along with two other pastors in the community. But for the fact that my role was limited to the reading of Scripture during the service, I might have been tempted to tell one of my favorite stories about two brothers. One died and the other made plans to bury his brother in a manner that honored the way he lived. Both brothers attended the same church. So, the surviving brother went to see their pastor and asked him to conduct the funeral. The pastor said yes. The surviving brother had only one request. "What is it?" the pastor asked. "Please, just tell everyone my brother was a saint!" the man replied.

The unusual request placed the pastor in a difficult position. He paused for a moment and then said, "You know I can't do that. Everyone knows your brother's terrible reputation. He was an immoral man, a liar, and a cheat. He cheated on his wife and family, cheated people in business, and he even cheated God out of the tithe. You want me to tell everyone he's a saint? I can't do that!"

That's when the surviving brother reached into his pocket and put a piece of paper on the desk. He then slid it across to the pastor. It was a check for $1 million made out to the church's building fund. The pastor took one look at all the zeroes on the check and said, "Let me see what I can do," and proceeded to put the check in a safe place.

The next day the pastor deposited the check in the bank as the first order of business and then drove to the church for the funeral. When it came time to speak about the deceased brother, the silver-tongued orator pulled no punches. He reminded everyone of the man's terrible reputation, calling him out as a liar and a cheat. He even said with a bit of glee, "I rarely saw him in church and today he meets his Maker!" The pastor glanced over at the surviving brother who by now was extremely agitated. That's when the pastor made good on his promise. He took a deep breath and said to the congregation with a loud voice, "But compared to his twin brother, this man was a saint!"

Okay, so I resisted the urge to tell that story at the funeral of the man who crashed his plane and duped his family. But when given the opportunity, I do always speak with candor about the final destination of the dead. Nothing does more to make us pause and think about what happens after death than a corpse in a casket. It's the ultimate object lesson for a preacher. One day every one of us will join with the dearly departed. It may happen suddenly like when an airplane crashes or as a result of a long illness. But make no mistake, your death and mine *will* arrive. And when it does, do you know your final destination?

The book you hold in your hand is a traveler's guide from here to eternity. Because life is preparation for eternity, the journey is as important as the destination. Along the way, as many questions exist about the afterlife as there are bodies in graves on planet earth. Some of those questions include:

- What happens sixty seconds after we die?
- Are heaven and hell real places?
- Is there a future resurrection and a final judgment?
- What about reincarnation, near-death experiences, and communicating with the dead?
- Is there a place called purgatory?
- Will we see our dead loved ones again in the hereafter?

And my personal favorite:

- Will my dog Fluffy reunite with me in heaven?

Everything we need to know about death and the afterlife is found in the pages of Scripture. Notice I said *need* to know, not *want* to know.

In his first letter to the Corinthians, the apostle Paul writes, "For now we see in a mirror dimly, but then face to face. Now I know in part; then I shall know fully, even as I have been fully known" (13:12). The New Living Translation says it this way: "Now we see things imperfectly, like puzzling reflections in a mirror, but then we will see everything with perfect clarity. All that I know now is partial and incomplete, but then I will know everything completely, just as God now knows me completely."

Imagine yourself traveling to New York City in November to watch the Macy's Thanksgiving Day Parade (something I've always wanted to do). You make your way to Fifth Avenue, but the crowds are so large that you get stuck behind an eight-foot-tall wooden fence. Your only view of the parade is through a knothole. Suddenly things go white and then black and then white again. You guess that it might be a giant balloon of Snoopy. That's sort of how we get to see the afterlife in this life. Sometimes God gives us nothing more than "puzzling reflections in a mirror" in the pages of Scripture. That means He chooses to leave some things in this life unanswered, and so must we as we walk by faith with Him toward our final destination.

In the meantime, we'll do anything to avoid the subject of death, won't we? Maybe that's because we fear the unknown. We live as though the inevitable will never happen to us. Or, perhaps we don't actually believe in the transcendent nature of life itself. Deep down inside we assume death is the end of all existence, and who wants to talk about that?

My thoughts and conclusions about the afterlife in this book aren't based on best guesses or on some special revelation I claim to have received, nor from a near-death or out-of-body experience.

Sensational stories about the hereafter abound, and they might create enough curiosity to sell many books, but they provide little more than false hope based on subjective experience. Any glimpse I share into the afterlife comes from the only reliable source we have for understanding things beyond the grave. The source I'm talking about is the Book of all books, the holy Bible.

I begin with the assumption that God exists and He has spoken to us through His written Word. He also came to this earth in the person of Jesus Christ, the Living Word. Fully God and fully human at the same time, Jesus lived a perfect life and died a real, painful death for us on a cross in order to fulfill His mission "to seek and to save the lost" (Luke 19:10). The most amazing thing about His life and death is that

He didn't remain in the grave. As He predicted, and as the Old Testament Scriptures prophesied, He rose from the dead to live forever. Jesus defeated the last enemy called death and laid claim to His own words: "I am the resurrection and the life" (John 11:25).

What this means to every human being on planet earth is profound: death has lost its sting and there's hope beyond the grave. If that doesn't make you shout hallelujah (and keep on reading), I don't know what will.

An Unexpected Passing

Recently, we experienced a death in our family. The Jones family dog died of an illness the veterinarian believed was cancer. Mandy was a sweet golden retriever we adopted through a Texas rescue agency when the kids were in grade school. Besides two tadpoles named Tad and Pole, and a goldfish my son named Elephant, we've never lost a family pet. It was a sad day and a grievous good-bye.

The doctors and nurses at the veterinary clinic across from a major university near where I live couldn't have been kinder. When I arrived to have Mandy euthanized, they were as sensitive as any pastor sitting with a family in the ICU. I know euthanasia is the humane thing we do for animals, but something about me deciding the day of Mandy's death didn't seem right. And it reinforced for me how wrong euthanasia is as a way to end a human life created in the image of God. As I left the clinic that day, the receptionist handed me what she called a "grief packet." It was stuffed with materials about "saying good-bye to a friend."

"Accepting the loss of your pet is necessary," it began. "Denial of your pain only prolongs the hurt." Okay, I understand how the death of a pet can cause emotional trauma in our lives. After almost ten years, Mandy really was part of our family. But as I read on, I was motivated even more to write this present book. "Just this side of heaven is a place called Rainbow Bridge. When an animal dies that has been especially close to someone here, that pet goes to Rainbow Bridge. There are meadows and hills for all our special friends so they can run and play together. There is plenty of food, water and sunshine, and our friends are warm and comfortable." It goes on to talk about the day when we will reunite with our pets and "cross the Rainbow Bridge together and walk into heaven."

Warm and sentimental? You bet. Comforting? Sure. But is it true? Where did they come up with the idea of the Rainbow Bridge? Another insert in the packet gave me a clue. It encouraged parents to view *The Lion King* movie with their children and teach them about "the circle of life." I was disappointed because the last place to form our theology about the afterlife is from a Disney movie. The film might be entertaining, but it reveals little about eternity.

So where are Fluffy, Mandy, Tad and Pole, Elephant, or for that matter, Simba? One of my professors in seminary was often asked this question and always answered it graciously. After waxing eloquently about the distinction between animals and humans who alone are created in the image of God, he would say with a slight smile, "However, if having Fluffy with you in heaven is necessary for your eternal happiness, I'm sure she'll be there!" My professor would always point us to the more important question related to the eternal destination of image-bearers like you and me.

Whenever I conduct a funeral, or when I read the grief materials handed out by well-meaning veterinarians, I'm reminded of how important it is to approach the subject of the afterlife with biblical accuracy and compassion. And that's what I promise you in the pages that follow. I'll do my best to write clearly when the Bible speaks clearly and remain silent when it's silent. When God's living and lasting Word leaves us looking through a mirror dimly, I won't attempt to clarify matters with my own speculation or point you to Hollywood for answers. Fair enough?

Whether you realize it or not, your journey toward your final destination began the day you were born. And the beginning of your discovery of what lies beyond the grave starts right now. I'm honored that you would pick up this traveler's guide and take the time to read it. I'm also praying that God will use it to awaken your understanding of the destiny for which He created you and the route to getting there.

2

Can We Really Live Forever?

Aubrey de Gray, age fifty-one, wants to live forever. He believes science is close to solving the problem of death through advanced technology and diet. At his research headquarters in Silicon Valley, de Gray told Charlotte Allen of *The Weekly Standard*, "Someone is alive right now who is going to live to be 1000 years old."[1]

Author of the 2007 book *Ending Aging,* de Gray is one of the leading spokespersons in the live-forever movement, espousing the tantalizing idea that death is not an inevitable part of the human condition. He places aging in the same category as heart disease and cancer—something to be cured. Scientists like de Gray are working hard to extend both the length of human life and its quality.

I have good news for the Cambridge-educated de Gray. He *will* live forever, but not on planet earth and not through advancements in science and technology. The Bible says we all are created in the image of God, and that makes us eternal beings (Genesis 1:26). Life continues after life here on earth. The question from the Bible's perspective is where will we spend eternity, in the blissful presence of our Creator or not?

According to the Bible, there was a time when human life on earth spanned hundreds of years. Noah, for example, lived to the ripe age of nine hundred fifty years, of which three hundred fifty came after the massive flood that covered the earth (Genesis 9:29). His grandfather, Methuselah, holds the world record for the longest living human being, which is why the phrase "as old as Methuselah" is common. Genesis 5:27 says, "Thus all the days of Methuselah were nine hundred sixty-nine years, and he died." Even Lamech, Noah's father, lived a relatively short life compared to his contemporaries. He died at the perfect age of seven hundred seventy-seven years.

But even a life span of nearly 1000 years is not *forever.* God created the first humans with the ability to live forever, placing Adam and Eve in a perfect locale called the Garden of Eden. He gave them everything they needed to enjoy life and each other. The Lord God of heaven and earth even took walks with Adam every day. It was truly paradise! But God also established moral boundaries for the first couple. He told them not to eat the fruit from the tree of the knowledge of good and evil or "you shall surely die" (Genesis 2:17).

It's uncertain whether Adam understood the true nature of death having never seen a life cut short. But when the first human chose to willfully disobey God's command, Adam and his wife Eve surely died, just as God said. They died spiritually and eventually physically. Like a Trojan virus attacking a laptop computer, sin corrupted the entire human race. Both our minds and our bodies were affected, shrinking our intellectual capacity and shortening our life span to something less than forever. Worse, sin severed our relationship with a holy God. Since then, "the whole creation has been groaning together in the pains of childbirth until now" (Romans 8:22). We were made for paradise, but we live in paradise lost.

The ten preflood patriarchs from Adam to Noah lived an average of nine hundred twelve years, excluding Enoch who did not die but was translated into God's presence at age three hundred sixty-five. However, during the 1000 years following the flood, human life spans on earth progressively declined. Abraham, for example, lived for one hundred seventy-five years. Moses lived for one hundred twenty years, which was long for his time. Near the end of his journey on earth, the leader of the Exodus reflected on the brevity of life by saying, "The years of our lives are seventy, or even by reason of strength eighty; yet their span is but toil and trouble; they are soon gone, and we fly away" (Psalm 90:10).

Today, life spans remain about the same. Life expectancy in the United States is around seventy-eight years while globally it's 67.2 years. People in Japan live the longest but only a few years longer than people in the U.S.[2] Despite advances in medical science and technology, the process of aging that leads to death is still a mystery, even to researchers like de Gray who are in search of immortality.

Much to de Gray's dismay and ours, death awaits us. As George Bernard Shaw once observed, "The statistics on death are really quite impressive. One out of one people die." We are not gods, angels, immortals, or superheroes. However, the Bible does speak of a day when we will shed our mortal clothing for immortality. After waxing eloquently about the resurrection of Jesus Christ, the apostle Paul writes these thought-provoking words to the Corinthians,

> For this perishable must put on the imperishable, and this mortal must put on immortality. But when this perishable will have put on the imperishable, and this mortal will have put on immortality, then will come about the saying that is written, 'Death is swallowed up in victory. O death, where is your victory? O death, where is your sting?' The sting of death is sin, and the power of sin is the law; but thanks be to God, who gives us the victory through our Lord Jesus Christ (1 Corinthians 15:53-57 NASB).

Can we really live forever? The Bible says yes, resoundingly! But not on our own. Not through science and technology. If victory ever swallows up death, it will not happen because of something we did or something new we discovered. Words like "death" and "victory" are possible in the same sentence only because of what Jesus accomplished for us on His cross and through His resurrection. He *gives us* the victory and removes the sting associated with death. That's the kind of good news that makes me shout, "Thanks be to God!"

3

Eternity in Our Hearts

Solomon, the son of King David, is widely regarded as the wisest man who ever lived, with the exception of wisdom's treasury embodied in the person of Jesus Christ. Solomon penned a book in the Bible's Old Testament called Ecclesiastes, a compilation of his personal reflections on life and his search for satisfaction. Solomon's favorite word is "vanity." He uses it nineteen times as a way of expressing the utter futility of trying to find purpose and meaning in life apart from the living God. The Lord knows Solomon tried.

In addition to wisdom, God gave Solomon untold wealth, making him the richest man who ever lived, even by the standards of today's billionaires. Possessing the greatest combination of intellectual, financial, and political resources available to one person, he used his advantages to enjoy life to the fullest. Whatever Solomon desired was within his reach, including seven hundred wives and three hundred concubines. He was a true icon, a human effigy ever-expanding his powerful kingdom, popularity, and prestige. The massive building projects he undertook, plus his vast depositories of gold and silver, even made the visiting Queen of Sheba feel small in his presence (1 Kings 10).

Solomon spent much of his time pondering his existence "under the sun," an expression he uses twenty-nine times in his search for the meaning of life. At times, his philosophical musings appear dark and gloomy. The emptiness of life overwhelms him. He learns firsthand how the pursuit of pleasure and power as an end in itself leaves a person desolate, carving out a hole in the human heart.

Fortunately, Solomon doesn't conclude his vain search for life's meaning in skepticism or atheism as many in our culture do today. His continual restlessness eventually led him to a wonderful discovery that he reveals at the end of his treatise, "Fear God and keep his commandments, for this is the whole duty of man" (Ecclesiastes 12:13). Along the way, Solomon also learns how God has wired the human heart in a way for him to discover the ultimate meaning in life. "He has made everything beautiful in its time," he writes in Ecclesiastes 3:11. "Also, he has put eternity into man's heart, yet so that he cannot find out what God has done from the beginning to the end."

Solomon sticks his head "above the sun" long enough to catch a glimpse of God and eternity. Beauty comes in understanding there's a purpose and meaning to everything under the sun. No matter how random life appears or painful it becomes, God is always up to something good and eternally appropriate for us. Earlier in chapter 3, Solomon writes eloquently about the rhythm of life, connecting the temporal with the eternal. "There is a time for every purpose under heaven," he begins in verse 1 (NKJV). What follows makes me tap my feet and burst into song. That's because in 1965 a popular folk-rock band called The Byrds made famous these biblical lyrics in a rhythmic tune called "Turn! Turn! Turn! (To Everything There Is a Season)." Solomon goes on to say,

> A time to be born, and a time to die; a time to plant, and a time to pluck what is planted; a time to kill, and a time to heal; a time to break down, and a time to build up; a time to weep, and a time to laugh; a time to mourn, and a time to dance; a time to cast away stones, and a time to gather stones; a time to embrace, and a time to refrain from embracing; a time to gain, and a time to lose; a time to keep, and a time to throw away; a time to tear, and a time to sew; a time to keep silence, and a time to speak; a time to

> love, and a time to hate; a time of war, and a time of peace (Ecclesiastes 3:2-8 NKJV).

It takes faith to believe God makes all things beautiful in His time, especially when tears and heartbreak define your present experience. That's when an eternal perspective—a view of life "above the sun"—helps tremendously. Solomon goes on to say God has "put eternity into man's heart." What does he mean by this? If there's something God has put in my heart with intention, I want to understand it.

The words of Thomas Watson, a Puritan pastor from yesteryear, provide some insight when he writes, "Eternity to the godly is a day that has no sunset; eternity to the wicked is a night that has no sunrise." In his book *The Bible Jesus Read,* acclaimed author Philip Yancey sees "eternity in our hearts" from another perspective by offering these thoughts:

> I once came across a scene of beauty outside Anchorage, Alaska. Against a slate-blue sky, the water of an ocean inlet had a slight greenish cast, interrupted by small whitecaps. Soon I saw these were not whitecaps at all but whales—silvery white beluga whales in a pod feeding no more than 50 feet offshore. I stood with other onlookers, listening to the rhythmic motion of the sea, following the graceful, ghostly crescents of surfacing whales. The crowd was hushed, even reverent. For just a moment, nothing else mattered.

Then Yancey adds, "The author of Ecclesiastes would have understood the crowd's response. He sees with dazzling clarity the beauty in the created world and that God 'has put eternity in their hearts.'"[3]

The fact that God's amazing creation can inspire a moment of worship as Yancey describes is one example of eternity in our hearts. But I believe there's more to this profound idea. From the very beginning God planned that you and I would live forever with Him. He put eternity in our hearts to remind us of that and to create in us a thirst for the transcendent. The meaninglessness of life evaporates when we know we are part of God's eternal plan and we allow that to become our focus.

Eternity, however, is a difficult concept to grasp. Try wrapping your brain around the word "forever" and you might pull a muscle in your mind. The fact that we are creatures bound by time and yet simultaneously created for eternity complicates our comprehension. We wear watches and carry digital calendars on our smart phones while, like Abraham, traveling toward an eternal city whose builder and maker is God (Hebrews 11:10 NKJV). While our tombstones mark the beginning and the end of a life with actual dates, we possess an innate sense that some kind of life continues after this life. The apostle Paul appropriately uses the word "groaning" to describe the restless yearning going on inside all of us. We groan for our redemption. Yes, even all of creation groans to rediscover the purpose for which God spoke the worlds into existence (Romans 8). As Augustine of Hippo famously said, "Thou hast made us for thyself, O Lord, and our heart is restless until it finds its rest in thee."[4]

Augustine also wrestled with the interplay of time and eternity. He asked, "How can the past and future be, when the past no longer is, and the future is not yet? As for the present, if it were always present and never moved on to become the past, it would not be time, but eternity."[5] It sounds like Augustine confused himself. Thinking about eternity makes our finite brains turn into cheese fondue.

The first words of the Bible found in Genesis 1 introduce us to the concept of eternity. The fact that God was present "in the beginning" suggests He existed before time began. Time and eternity may not be linear concepts exactly, but here's how my finite mind reasons. For grins, imagine climbing into your DeLorean time machine and traveling back in time as far as you can. There you'll find God perched on the edge of time and eternity. Then turn around and travel forward in time—back to the future, as it were—until days, weeks, months, and years spill over into forever. There you will also find God. Having never not existed, God created something out of nothing. Rewind that last sentence and read it again slowly.

While reflecting on the brevity of his own life in Psalm 90, Moses begins with creation and quickly bumps into eternity, "Before the mountains were brought forth, or ever you had formed the earth and the world, from everlasting to everlasting you are God" (v. 2). "From everlasting to everlasting"—now there's a concept! As Winston Churchill once quipped, it sounds like "a riddle, wrapped in a mystery, inside an enigma." Or, as one of my favorite theologians named Buzz Lightyear often says, "To infinity and beyond!"

According to Solomon, God put a small part of "infinity and beyond" in the human heart, but not enough for us to completely fathom the Lord Almighty's plans from beginning to end. The Hebrew word translated "eternity" comes from another word that means "to hide." Is God hiding something from us? He certainly placed within each of us an innate awareness and curiosity about the afterlife. Perhaps that's why you're reading this book. But He didn't tell us everything. By God's design and divine prerogative, some things about the afterlife remain a mystery. We will never know all we want to know about life beyond until we arrive there. Until then, we walk by faith.

If left unguarded, that curiosity within can lead us down a dark and dangerous pathway into New Age mysticism, deception, and the occult. However, it doesn't have to. It can and should lead us into the brilliant light of God's presence. He alone reveals the mysteries of life after life in His holy and trustworthy Word called the Bible. God has already told us what we need to know about the afterlife, nothing more or less. The exhilarating exploration of that knowledge lies in the pages ahead. But first we must face an unpleasant enemy.

4

The Last Enemy

The Bible is primarily a book about life not death. Read God's Word from beginning to end and you'll find the tree of life, not the tree of death, appearing in both Genesis and Revelation. When God created man in His own image, "the Lord God formed the man of dust from the ground and breathed into his nostrils the breath of life, and the man became a living creature" (Genesis 2:7). Later, Moses urged the people of Israel to "choose life" as they prepared to cross the Jordan River and take possession of the Promised Land (Deuteronomy 30:19). God has a free gift He wants to give to you and me; it's called eternal life (Romans 6:23). Even Jesus said, "I have come that you might have life and have it abundantly" (John 10:10, paraphrase). Life is everywhere in the Bible.

And so, every time I conduct a funeral, I think, *Something is not right about this. It wasn't supposed to be this way. Death is a rude interruption to the life God meant for us.* But death is a real part of life as we know it. So, let's review how and why death invaded our world.

Death is the consequence of sin according to Romans 6:23, which reads, "The wages of sin is death." Make no mistake about it, transgressing God's laws (the definition of sin) yields a painful payday! Earlier in Romans, the apostle Paul writes, "Therefore, just as sin came into the world through one man, and death through sin, and so death spread to all men because all sinned" (Romans 5:12). This explains the origin of the evil nature inside every human heart. The "one man" mentioned in this verse is Adam from whom we inherited a sin nature. The first mention of death is found in the creation story located in the early chapters of Genesis. Let's go back to the beginning for a closer look.

> The LORD God took the man and put him in the garden of Eden to work it and keep it. And the LORD God commanded the man, saying, "You may surely eat of every tree of the garden, but of the tree of the knowledge of good and evil you shall not eat, for in the day that you eat of it you shall surely die" (Genesis 2:15-17).

Genesis is critical to our understanding of so many Christian doctrines, including the nature of man, the origin of death, and the consequences of sin. The book of beginnings tells us God created man in His own image and then drew moral boundaries for him. He placed two special trees in the Garden of Eden. One was called the tree of life and the other was called the tree of the knowledge of good and evil. God gave Adam the freedom of choice but restricted him from eating the fruit produced from the tree of the knowledge of good and evil. The consequences of eating the forbidden fruit was certain death—"You shall surely die," the Lord said to Adam. The point is we are free moral beings who can choose to obey God or not, but we cannot choose our consequences.

I find it interesting that the first recorded lie the devil ever told was about death. Satan approached Adam's wife in the form of a slithering serpent and began questioning God's word. "You shall not surely die," he said in contrast to what God had said. Notice how the devil twisted God's word ever-so-slightly by adding the small, three-letter word "not." The serpent placed enough doubt in Eve's mind that she also began questioning God's word. Eventually she persuaded Adam to follow her lead. They ate the forbidden fruit and the rest is our shared history. No doubt Jesus had this scene in mind when He calls the devil "a liar and the father of lies" (John 8:44). If the devil can get us to believe a lie about death and the afterlife, he's halfway home to achieving his diabolical goal of distorting the reality of our true spiritual condition.

After they disobeyed God, Adam and Eve were immediately banished from paradise. One could argue this was an expression of God's grace. By deporting the first humans from the Garden of Eden, God protected them from eating from the tree of life, which would have sealed their fate as unredeemed sinners in rebellion against their Creator. Furthermore, had Adam not died, he would have lived forever in his sinful state. Death became part of God's plan only after humankind rebelled against Him.

The next time the tree of life appears is in the new heaven and earth (Revelation 22). This is why some say the Bible tells the story of paradise, paradise lost, and paradise regained.

The Separation of Body and Soul

So, what exactly is death? A clear definition depends on your view of the nature of human beings. If we are physical beings only, then the clinical definition of death is sufficient. Medically speaking, death is the cessation of all vital bodily functions including breathing, heartbeat, and brain activity. However, the Bible teaches that man is a unified being with both material and immaterial aspects.

Those who deny the existence of God and the afterlife want us to believe we are physical beings only, evolved from an unlikely series of experiments resulting from a mixture of chance and time. However, I actually believe we are purposely created beings. We are spiritual beings living in a material world.

Much debate exists among theologians about the nature of the immaterial part of us. Are we dichotomous or trichotomous beings? Dichotomy refers to body and soul whereas trichotomy differentiates between the body, soul, and spirit. Though a few texts exist in Scripture that seem to support the threefold view of humans (1 Thessalonians 5:23; Hebrews 4:12; 1 Corinthians 14:14), I believe the weight of biblical evidence backs the idea that we are dichotomous beings, variously referred to in the New Testament as body and soul (Matthew 10:28), body and spirit (1 Corinthians 7:34; James 2:26), body and mind (Romans 12:1-2), flesh and spirit (Romans 8:1-11; Galatians 5:22-25), outer man and inner man (2 Corinthians 4:16). For that reason, I will use the words "spirit" and "soul" interchangeably throughout this book.

Why does it matter whether we possess a body and soul or a body, soul, and spirit? Hank Hanegraaff of the Christian Research Institute suggests, "The trichotomist view is typically used to support the idea that God communicates mystically with our spirits and thus bypasses our intellects. Remember, the heart cannot fully rejoice in what the mind does not comprehend, and this false teaching leads people to swallow other false and destructive heresies as well."[6]

At the end of the day, it matters significantly that we are more than mere physical beings that evolved over time in a purely material world. Whether dichotomous or trichotomous, we were created in the image of God to live forever and have a relationship with Him. As unified beings, we relate to God with both our body and spirit. In fact, one of the ways we know we are rightly related to God is when "the Spirit himself bears witness with our spirit that we are children of God" (Romans 8:16). Later in the same book of Romans, Paul says to "present your bodies as a living sacrifice, holy and acceptable to God" (12:1).

This understanding of human nature leads us to an entirely different definition of death. The Bible defines death as the separation of the immaterial from the material or the spirit from the body. For example, James 2:26 says, "For as the body apart from the spirit is dead, so also faith apart from works is dead." In the Old Testament, Isaac's wife Rachel died while giving birth to her second son, Benjamin. Genesis 35:18 describes her death as her soul departing from her body. Likewise, when Jesus raised Jairus's daughter from the dead, we read, "her spirit returned" to her body (Luke 8:55). Luke was a well-schooled physician and, surprisingly, he avoided using medical terms to describe the girl's death and return to life.

Our body, then, is the temporary dwelling place of our spirit or soul. The apostle Paul has this in mind when he writes, "For we know that if the tent that is our earthly home is destroyed, we have a building from God, a house not made with hands, eternal in the heavens. For in this tent we groan, longing to put on our heavenly dwelling" (2 Corinthians 5:1-2).

Paul's tent analogy is worth exploring further. Compared to a brick-and-mortar home, a tent is a weak, frail, vulnerable, and temporary dwelling place. I know that is true because I'm not much of a camper and when I put up a tent, it usually falls down. That's when I groan! A tent is also an apt description of our physical bodies. Apparently we are all just camping out in these bodies of ours. As I write these words, I'm feeling the flimsy nature of my own physical tent because of pain in my lower back. Yes, I'm groaning because my body doesn't work as well as it once did. But one day I will die and my spirit will leave this old tent behind.

Biblically, death is the departure of the soul from the body. Near the time of his own death, the apostle Paul wrote, "I am already being poured out as a drink offering, and the time of my departure has come" (2 Timothy 4:6). Elsewhere in his letter to the Philippians, he said, "If I am to go on living in the body, this will mean fruitful labor for me. Yet what shall I choose? I do not know! I am torn between the two: I desire to *depart and be with Christ*, which is better by far" (Philippians 1:22-23 NIV). Stephen, the first martyr of the church, had this same departure in mind when he prayed, "Lord Jesus, receive my spirit" (Acts 7:59). And consider the "second death," mentioned only once in Revelation 20:1. It refers to the separation of the soul from the presence of God forever.

When my wife Cathryn's father died several years ago, he was at home with hospice care. The kind hospice nurse encouraged the family to come near and remain in the room when my father-in-law passed from this life into the next. She said it was often her experience to actually feel the dying person's spirit leave the body. She said at the moment it happens, a slight change in the dead person's facial appearance will take place. She was right. It was ever so slight, but Cathryn witnessed a change in her father's countenance the moment he died and his body became an empty tent.

When vital bodily functions cease, the spirit leaves the body and lives on in eternity. Days later our physical body goes into the grave, more often than not, and awaits a future resurrection. What happens sixty seconds after we die? In short, we are disembodied spirits existing in the presence of God or in a place of unimaginable torment. More on that later. For now, it's time to talk about an appointment that's already been made for us.

5

Your Appointment with Death

Did you hear the story about two friends who shared a love for the game of baseball? One of the friends died and went to heaven. The other friend grieved the loss of his baseball buddy and then wondered if they'd play the game together in the afterlife. One day the dead friend appeared to his grieving friend in a dream. He said, "I have good news and bad news for you. The good news is there is baseball in heaven. The bad news is you're scheduled as the starting pitcher this Thursday night."

There's no indication in Scripture we'll play baseball in heaven, but I do know this: death is inevitable. The Bible says in Hebrews 9:27, "It is appointed for man to die once, and after that comes judgment." The fact that we "die once" speaks of the sureness of death. It also negates the idea that our lives recycle after death through reincarnation. The Bible always points us to the hope of a future resurrection not reincarnation, a belief found in Buddhism and other Eastern religions. That's why this present earthly life is truly preparation for eternity. We have one opportunity to get right with God and live for Him.

Ecclesiastes 3:1-2 says, "For everything there is a season, a time for every matter under heaven: a time to be born, and a time to die." We don't know the appointed time of our own death, but God does. He made the appointment for us. Use your sanctified imagination to think about a calendar in heaven that has your appointed time of death written down. Sobering thought, isn't it?

Current estimates are that more than 90 million people die every year on planet earth. That means nearly 250,000 people die every day, 10,000 every hour, one hundred seventy every minute. Approximately three people die every second of every day. No wonder Bill O'Reilly of *The O'Reilly Factor* says life after death is a "huge business in America!"[7] It is!

Benjamin Franklin is credited with saying "There are only two certainties in life—death and taxes." I respectfully disagree with Mr. Franklin for two reasons. First, a good accountant can reduce your taxes to near zero. I heard recently that 43 percent of Americans pay no income taxes at all. So that leaves us with the certainty of death. We've already established that "it is appointed for man to die once." However, there are exceptions. Neither Enoch nor Elijah the prophet experienced death. They were both translated into God's presence. Also, the Bible speaks of a generation of believers in Jesus Christ that will escape the experience of death altogether. They are the ones living on earth when Jesus returns for His church. In his first letter to the Corinthians, the apostle Paul writes about a future event in Bible prophecy known as the rapture of the church. He calls it a "mystery"—something that was once concealed but is now revealed in Scripture.

> Behold! I tell you a mystery. We shall not all sleep, but we shall all be changed, in a moment, in the twinkling of an eye, at the last trumpet. For the trumpet will sound, and the dead will be raised imperishable, and we shall be changed (1 Corinthians 15:51-52).

Paul uses the word "sleep" as a euphemism for death. This is not a reference to "soul sleep" as some suggest but refers to how the body looks when the spirit departs at the moment of death. However, "we shall not all sleep." Some believers will be alive when Jesus returns for His church. As fast as the eye blinks, Jesus will snatch His church off the face of the earth. Can you imagine the complete chaos as millions of people suddenly disappear from this world? First Thessalonians 4:16-17 describes this moment in greater detail by revealing, "The dead in Christ will rise first. Then we who are alive, who are left, will be caught up together with them in the clouds to meet the Lord in the air, and so we will always be with the Lord." These are encouraging words for all true believers in Jesus Christ. In short, some people will not experience death because they are alive when Jesus returns for His church.

So, if you want to avoid the certainty of death and taxes, find yourself a good accountant and then make sure you're a believer in Jesus Christ and alive when He returns for His church. Of course, the "alive when He returns" part is easier said than done. Nobody knows the day or the hour of Jesus's coming, so we must simultaneously prepare for death and His imminent return.

The Death of Death

Bob Mankoff is the cartoon editor for *The New Yorker* magazine. His job is a laugh-a-minute. *The New Yorker* has published more than 80,000 cartoons since its first issue. In an interview he did with *60 Minutes* correspondent Morley Safer, Mankoff said the Grim Reaper has appeared in the magazine's funny pages more than any other character. For example, in a recent David Sipress cartoon, the Reaper's latest acquisition is saying: "Thank goodness you're here—I can't accomplish anything unless I have a deadline."

"Honestly, if it wasn't for death. I don't think there'd be any humor," says Mankoff with a Cheshire cat-like grin on his face. He concludes the interview with Safer with these temporal but hope-filled words: "Grim Reaper's gonna get the last laugh. Until then, it's our turn."[8]

I'm glad Mankoff can laugh at death until the Reaper gets, in his opinion, the last laugh. However, I have better news for him. One day, death itself will die. The Grim Reaper will be fired, never to make another acquisition. He doesn't get the last laugh after all, at least not for the believer in Jesus Christ. The promise of Scripture is that Jesus must reign "until he has put all his enemies under his feet. The last enemy to be destroyed is death" (1 Corinthians 15:25-26). Rewind that last sentence and read it again. *The last enemy to be destroyed is death.* Jesus did not merely defeat death through His cross and resurrection; one day He will destroy it altogether! A thrilling glimpse into the end of the age through the lens of Bible prophecy reveals the truth of this statement.

The Bible predicts a day when Jesus Christ will return to this earth and defeat His enemies. Following a final world conflict that takes place in the Valley of Megiddo, also known as Armageddon, the victor Jesus will establish His kingdom reign on earth for one thousand years. The saints will inherit the earth while Jesus's prayer "Thy kingdom come, Thy will be done, in earth as it is in heaven" is literally fulfilled (Matthew 6:10 KJV). Satan, the ancient serpent, will also be bound during this time so that he cannot deceive the nations.

At the end of this time Bible scholars call the Millennium, Satan will be loosed from the bottomless pit for a brief season. He will deceive the nations one last time and gather armies from the four corners of the earth to fight against the saints of God and Jerusalem, the beloved holy city. That's when fire from heaven will consume the devil and he will be thrown into the lake of fire with the beast and the false prophet to be "tormented day and night forever and ever" (Revelation 20:10). The Bible reads better than any Hollywood script about the end of the world.

What follows in the book of Revelation is a sobering description of something called the Great White Throne Judgment. In his vision, the apostle John saw "the dead, great and small, standing before the throne...and the dead were judged" (v. 12). The apostle whom Jesus loved goes on to say, "Death and Hades gave up the dead who were in them, and they were judged, each one of them, according to what they had done. Then Death and Hades were thrown into the lake of fire. This is the second death, the lake of fire" (vv. 13-14).

This is also the death of death, or the time when the last enemy, death itself, is destroyed once and for all. And who makes this incredible feat happen? Who stands alone as the Judge of all the earth? Who finally dumps the Grim Reaper into the lake of fire where he can no longer threaten our peace? You guessed it. The resurrected Jesus. John concludes the Revelation of Jesus Christ by describing the new heaven and the new earth as a place where "death shall be no more" (21:4).

Pour over those last four words again and again until they steep in your soul like a teabag in hot water. No more death. Doesn't that sound great? Say it aloud. *No more death.* Now truly that's something for the heaven-bound believer in Jesus to laugh about.

6

Between Death and the Future Resurrection

I grew up in Indiana, so you can imagine my keen interest when I heard about a cemetery located somewhere in the Hoosier state where one of the tombstones read, "Pause, stranger, when you pass me by. As you are now, so once was I. As I am now, so you will be. So prepare for death and follow me."

Someone walked by that tombstone and scratched a snarky reply that said, "To follow you I'm not content, until I know which way you went."[9]

Curiosity about the afterlife abounds, dating back to the time of Job. Many people believe the book of Job is the oldest book in the Bible. If true, man's inquisitiveness about life after life enjoys a long history. During his unimaginable and personal suffering, Job contemplated death by asking an enigmatic question, "But a man dies and is laid low; man breathes his last, and where is he?" A few verses later, Job asks bluntly, "If man dies, shall he live again?" (Job 14:10,14)

Will the dead live again? If so, where are the dead now? These are the questions of the ages. Is there any way of knowing where our dead loved ones are, or whether we will see them again in the next life? Does the Bible tell us anything we can know for sure about the afterlife?

And, did Jesus say anything about the dead? Let's take a closer look at Scripture.

Jesus once told a story about two men from vastly different backgrounds. One was poor and the other was insanely rich. Both died at the same time, but each had a different experience in the afterlife. Their story is recorded in Luke 16:19-31 and gives us a glimpse into what happens sixty seconds after we die. It's worth reading from start to finish, slowly and carefully.

> There was a rich man who was clothed in purple and fine linen and who feasted sumptuously every day. And at his gate was laid a poor man named Lazarus, covered with sores, who desired to be fed with what fell from the rich man's table. Moreover, even the dogs came and licked his sores. The poor man died and was carried by the angels to Abraham's side. The rich man also died and was buried, and in Hades, being in torment, he lifted up his eyes and saw Abraham far off and Lazarus at his side. And he called out, "Father Abraham, have mercy on me, and send Lazarus to dip the end of his finger in water and cool my tongue, for I am in anguish in this flame." But Abraham said, "Child, remember that you in your lifetime received your good things, and Lazarus in like manner bad things; but now he is comforted here, and you are in anguish. And besides all this, between us and you a great chasm has been fixed, in order that those who would pass from here to you may not be able, and none may cross from there to us." And he said, "Then I beg you, father, to send him to my father's house—for I have five brothers—so that he may warn them, lest they also come into this place of torment." But Abraham said, "They have Moses and the Prophets; let them hear them." And he said, "No, father Abraham, but if someone goes to them from the dead, they will repent." He said to him, "If they do not hear Moses and the Prophets, neither will they be convinced if someone should rise from the dead."

One of the reasons Jesus told this story was to remind the greedy

Pharisees that economic status has no bearing on one's final destination. Earlier in verse 14, Luke writes, "The Pharisees, who were lovers of money, heard all these things and they ridiculed him." What things? Things like "you cannot serve God and money." The Pharisees coiled up like rattlesnakes whenever Jesus hit close to home with His teaching, and in this case He did.

Money is not a sign of God's favor, as the Pharisees believed it was. Nor is the lack of money an indication you are destined for the flames of hell. How ridiculous to think that way. In this life, it takes a lot of money to travel with your family to an island paradise in the Caribbean. But wealth has no ability to buy you a trip to paradise in the next life, nor does the lack of it prevent you from going there. The reversal in the story Jesus told should rattle the attention of those who believe prosperity is a ticket to paradise. The rich man went to a place of torment called Hades and the poor man went to paradise, called Abraham's bosom in the story. Make no mistake about it. We cannot buy our way into heaven nor should we trust riches to get us there.

Some people believe this story Jesus told says nothing specific about the afterlife, choosing to include it among His many parables. I disagree. Parables are general stories that communicate general principles. They usually refer to "a certain man" who travels to "a certain place." Particulars are conspicuously absent in parables. However, the story Jesus told about a rich man and Lazarus is different from a parable. It mentions specific people and specific places, leaving most Bible scholars (including me) with the impression Jesus is referring to something He knew actually happened in the afterlife. If that's true, the story of the rich man and Lazarus provides us with the most trustworthy glimpse into life beyond the grave ever recorded.

"And in Hades"

To fully understand this story and its profound implications, we must clarify several terms used here and elsewhere in Scripture. They include Sheol, Hades, Gehenna, hell, lake of fire, second death, Abraham's bosom, and paradise. Though sometimes tedious, it's worth taking a closer look at the terms and conditions related to the afterlife, beginning with two of the most common ones appearing in the Old and New Testaments.

Verse 23 identifies the location of the rich man and Lazarus as a place called Hades. Sheol and Hades are essentially one and the same place, the temporary abode of departed spirits. In the Greek translation of the Old Testament called the Septuagint, the Hebrew word Sheol is rendered "Hades." The time spent in Sheol (or Hades) is what theologians refer to as the intermediate state.

In the thirty-nine books of the Old Covenant, Sheol is the most important word related to the afterlife. It first appears in Genesis 37:35 where Jacob expresses deep grief after his sons deceived him into believing their youngest brother, Joseph, had been killed by wild animals. "All his sons and all his daughters rose up to comfort him, but he refused to be comforted and said, 'No, I shall go down to Sheol to my son, mourning.' Thus his father wept for him."

Old Testament saints like Jacob always thought of Sheol as being located down in some lower part of the earth. Job, for example, writes, "As the cloud fades and vanishes, so he who goes down to Sheol does not come up" (7:9) and "in peace they go down to Sheol" (21:13). The writer of Proverbs refers to Sheol in a warning about associating with a prostitute by saying, "Her house is the way to Sheol, going down to the chambers of death" (Proverbs 7:27). In other words, down, down, down goes anybody who chases after a woman of ill repute. The prophet Isaiah also weighs in on Sheol, providing us with a fascinating insight into the stirring activity and conversation that takes place there.

> Sheol beneath is stirred up to meet you when you come; it rouses the shades to greet you, all who were leaders of the earth; it raises from their thrones all who were kings of the nations. All of them will answer and say to you: "You too have become as weak as we! You have become like us!" (Isaiah 14:9-10).

Sheol appears sixty-five times throughout the Hebrew Scriptures and is variously translated "hell," "grave," "pit," and "death." However, some of these translations are misleading. For example, in the King James Version of the Bible, some believe the king's scholars incorrectly used the word "hell" to translate Sheol. Neither Sheol in the Old Testament nor Hades in the New Testament is the actual place called hell. The major difference is that Sheol (or Hades) is the temporary residence of departed spirits while hell is a permanent place of torment for the wicked dead. And while both Sheol and Hades can refer generally to the grave or pit, they are never that alone.

That said, nobody actually inhabits hell right now, not even Adolph Hitler, Saddam Hussein, Osama bin Laden, or the most evil person you can imagine. According to Revelation 20:13-14, as God adjudicates the wicked dead at the Great White Throne Judgment (a future event in Bible prophecy), death and Hades relinquish their captives and then they are thrown into the lake of fire, a place synonymous with hell. This is also called the "second death." Until then, the wicked dead remain in torment in Hades. Think of Hades as the Guantanamo Bay of the afterlife, only there is no waterboarding, cable television with ESPN, or the hope of getting released to a better place. What awaits those waiting there is something far more horrifying.

The scene recorded near the end of John's apocalypse is one of the most sobering found anywhere in Scripture. One can hardly read it without shedding tears of compassion for those, great and small, who are forever banished from the presence of God Almighty. Kings and peasants, presidents and peons, corporate titans and blue collar workers, even patriots and selfish pinheads are cast away for one reason only: "If anyone's name was not found written in the book of life, he was thrown into the lake of fire" (Revelation 20:15).

This should provide Christ followers all of the motivation we need to share the good news of Jesus Christ's salvation with our family, friends, neighbors, and strangers. It also begs the most important question of all time: is your name written in the book of life? When you pass from this life to the next, will people from the Hoosier state—or wherever you are from—know which way you went?

Now, let's return to Luke 16 and take a closer look at what Jesus says happens to us moments after we die.

7

Sixty Seconds After We Die

In his book *Baseball Through a Knothole,* Bill Borst tells the story of a generous St. Louis insurance man named W.E. Bilheimer. He made it possible for the city's youth to attend a professional baseball game who otherwise couldn't afford a ticket. Back then and long before today's super stadiums, ballparks were built with wooden fences. Kids who didn't have tickets gathered in the outfield and watched the game through knotholes in the fence. It wasn't the best view of the game, but it was better than no view at all. Glimpses of baseball greats like Dizzy Dean and Leo Durocher kept the kids coming back. They became known as the "knothole gang."

As part of a fan syndicate, Bilheimer provided a free bleacher seat for the city's youth whenever someone purchased $50 of stock in the Cardinal franchise. In time, the idea caught on. Knothole Gang Clubs with free and special-priced tickets for youth began popping up all over Major League Baseball. My father-in-law grew up in St. Louis in the 1930s and was part of the knothole gang. He was also a lifelong fan of the St. Louis Cardinals.

In the Old Testament, Sheol is like looking into the afterlife through a knothole. If all we knew about the afterlife was from the

Old Testament, we would see only glimpses of shadows, or "puzzling reflections in a mirror" as Paul says in 1 Corinthians 13:12 (NLT). However, a shift takes place in the New Testament. Theologians attribute it to the progress of revelation when Jesus throws the door to the afterlife wide open. With his story in Luke 16 about two men who died and went to Hades, Jesus invites us inside and provides, as it were, bleacher seats for the knothole gang. Let's take a closer look.

The Old Testament hints at something that gains clarity in the New Testament. Prior to Jesus's death, resurrection, and ascension, both the righteous and the unrighteous go to Hades (or Sheol) upon death. Some changes take place after Jesus returns to the Father. We'll discuss those changes later. For now, let's stay focused on Luke 16:22-31 where it appears Hades has two compartments separated by a great chasm or gulf. One is a place of torment and the other is a place of bliss called Abraham's bosom, a Jewish reference to paradise. In the story, the rich man, to the surprise of the Pharisees, travels to the place of torment while poverty-stricken Lazarus lands in Abraham's bosom. Quite a reversal of fortune.

FULL CONSCIOUSNESS

The first insight we gain from the story in Luke chapter 16 is that sixty seconds after we die we are fully conscious in the afterlife. In verses 22-24, Jesus says,

> "The rich man also died and was buried, and in Hades, being in torment, he lifted up his eyes and saw Abraham far off, and Lazarus at his side. And he called out, 'Father Abraham, have mercy on me, and send Lazarus to dip the end of his finger in water and cool my tongue, for I am in anguish in this flame.' "

Merriam-Webster defines consciousness as "the quality or state of being aware; the normal state of being awake and able to understand what is happening around you." This certainly describes the rich man in Hades. He lifts up his eyes and sees Lazarus off in the distance, has a conversation with Abraham, and feels pain. All of this points to the fact that he is fully aware of his surroundings. Even more to the point, four of his five senses are still operational. The only one of his five senses not at work in the story is smell.

- Sight—"He lifted up his eyes and saw Abraham far off"
- Hearing—"And he called out"... "But Abraham said" (v. 25)
- Taste—"Dip the end of his finger in water and cool my tongue"
- Touch—"Being in torment"... "I am in anguish in this flame"

One author says, "In hades, an alcoholic will thirst for a drop of liquor, but none will be given to him. The drug addict will crave a shot of heroin, but will not receive it. The immoral man will burn with sexual desire, but never be satisfied."[10] This is true for the unrighteous dead. The righteous dead enjoy an opposite experience. Their deepest desires are perfectly satisfied in the afterlife.

In the paradise part of Hades, the righteous dead experience untold bliss. Jesus describes Lazarus as having once experienced "bad things," but now he is "comforted" at Abraham's side. Picture John the disciple leaning against Jesus in the Upper Room during the Passover meal and you catch a glimpse of how Lazarus positions himself next to Abraham. We can also imagine that all five of his senses were heightened in a way that he experienced intellectual, emotional, and spiritual euphoria. After the resurrection of the righteous dead when we receive our new, improved, and eternal bodies, physical euphoria will be our experience and his. More on that in a later chapter.

Jehovah's Witnesses and Seventh-day Adventists deny that we experience consciousness in the afterlife, suggesting we lose awareness at death and the soul basically sleeps until the resurrection of the dead. This false teaching known as "soul sleep" is found in some of the non-canonical writings of the early church and is based on a misunderstanding of Paul's use of the word "sleep" in 1 Corinthians 15:51-52 and 1 Thessalonians 4:13-14.

It's true the word "sleep" often appears in Scripture as a synonym of death. For example, Jesus told His disciples, "Our friend Lazarus has fallen asleep, but I go to awaken him" (John 11:11). Matthew writes about a great earthquake that took place during Jesus's crucifixion and how "the tombs also were opened. And many bodies of the saints who had fallen asleep were raised" (Matthew 27:52). However, as I mentioned earlier, "sleep" in reference to death is always a description of the way the body appears as a corpse, not to what the soul is doing. As one author says, "It is the *body*, not the soul, that 'sleeps' in death."[11]

PAINFUL TORMENT

You've heard the phrase, "You can't have one without the other." Well, in the Bible, there's no heaven without hell; there's no eternal life without eternal punishment. In Luke 16 and elsewhere, Jesus describes a place of unimaginable torment and suffering. Both Hades and hell are real places where real people experience real and eternal pain. That is not to say God runs a cosmic torture chamber. I believe there's a slight but important difference between torture and torment. Torture happens against a person's will while torment is self-inflicted. Torment is the mental and physical anguish that results from our own sinful choices. Think of hell (or temporarily Hades) as a place where the painful consequences of a person's free moral choices apart from God are fully and eternally realized without the hope of forgiveness or redemption. Those in agony will have nobody to blame but themselves.

Haunting memories are part of the painful torment the wicked experience in Hades. When the rich man cries out for relief, Abraham says, "Child, remember that you in your lifetime received your good things, and Lazarus in like manner bad things; but now he is comforted here, and you are in anguish" (Luke 16:25).

As we get older, our memories fade. I've always had to write things down and use helpful memory techniques, but these days I tend to remember the things I should forget and forget the things I should remember. Tragically, some people fall prey to dementia and eventually Alzheimer's disease, which erases one's memory and cognitive abilities altogether. Some of us practice selective Alzheimer's by trying to suppress the painful memories of the past. However, suppression is only a temporary solution and, at best, an emotional Band-Aid. In the afterlife, the memory of the wicked will return in full. Hades rips off the Band-Aid and forces the unrighteous dead to remember, at least, the opportunities they squandered to exercise faith in Jesus Christ. Perhaps there's no greater pain in hell than regret.

The Bible is less clear about the memory of believers in eternity. While I believe followers of Jesus will recognize each other in heaven, the Bible also says God will wipe away every tear (Revelation 21:4). What we do know is there is no sorrow or pain in heaven. The memories in this life that produced relational tension, bitterness, and remorse will not exist in heaven. But what about the memory of family and friends who rejected Jesus Christ and are experiencing eternal torment in hell? Will we remember them? If yes, how will that happen without filling our hearts with deep sorrow?

Isaiah 65:17 (NIV) seems to suggest God will modify our memories in the afterlife. The Lord says, "See, I will create new heavens and a new earth. The former things will not be remembered, nor will they come to mind." The extent of the "former things" not remembered remains a mystery. But as believers we can assume we will not remember anything that produces sorrow, including the memory of lost loved ones who are suffering in hell.

Fixed Destiny

Perhaps Jesus's most haunting words about the afterlife are found in Luke 16:26-31. Abraham says to the wealthy man suffering in Hades,

> " 'And besides all this, between us and you a great chasm has been fixed, in order that those who would pass from here to you may not be able, and none may cross from there to us.' And he said, 'Then I beg you, father, to send him to my father's house—for I have five brothers—so that he may warn them, lest they also come into this place of torment.' But Abraham said, 'They have Moses and the Prophets; let

> them hear them.' And he said, 'No, father Abraham, but if someone goes to them from the dead, they will repent.' He said to him, 'If they do not hear Moses and the Prophets, neither will they be convinced if someone should rise from the dead.'"

"None may cross from there to us." Those words mean the same in the Greek language as they do in English, and they imply a fixed destiny. They should make each of us pause and ponder our own eternal destiny as well as the final destination of all human beings. Some believe the unrighteous will get a second chance to change their minds, repent of their sins, and turn to God in the afterlife. However, Jesus made it clear this is not possible. He used the word "fixed" to describe the great distance between the rich man and Lazarus.

I understand how difficult it is to accept the eternal punishment of the wicked. Nobody in his or her right mind takes joy in the thought of it. Something inside of us recoils at the kind of torment that lasts forever. Did I say *forever*? We would rather God, at some point, offer clemency to suffering sinners, wouldn't we? This is why some venture into either universalism or annihilationism and ignore what Jesus clearly teaches.

Annihilationists believe the flames of hell will eventually extinguish all wicked souls, making any torment in the afterlife temporary. Universalists, on the other hand, cling to the love of God and believe everyone will eventually end up in heaven. They reason, people who die and find themselves in hell ("Whatever that is," they would say) don't have to stay there. They get a second chance to repent. And who wouldn't change his mind, if given the chance, after spending as few as sixty seconds in unimaginable torment? Rob Bell, the popular author and former pastor of Mars Hill Church in Michigan, is the latest to advocate for universalism in his controversial book *Love Wins.* He imagines in the afterlife, "The love of God will melt every hard heart, even the most 'depraved sinners' will eventually give up their resistance and turn to God."[12] The problem is Bell and other universalists must truncate biblical authority and ignore or deny the clear words of Jesus in order to come to this "more acceptable" conclusion.

When the rich man learns there is no crossing over in Hades, he begs Abraham to send Lazarus to warn his siblings of the terrible fate that awaits those who reject God in this life. The only explanation for his sense of urgency is the fact that he now clearly understands there are no second chances after death. His compassion for his five brothers is noteworthy. He doesn't want them to suffer too. He thinks perhaps a message from a dead person will change their thinking. However, he is told that if his brothers don't respond to the revelation they have been given (Moses and the Prophets), more revelation (the resurrection of the dead) won't persuade them because their hearts are hardened.

The phrase "if someone should rise from the dead" was probably a cryptic reference made by Jesus to His own future resurrection while foreshadowing the calcified response of so many human beings.

What about you? Is your heart still too stony to place your faith in the risen Christ despite the evidence of the empty tomb?

Contrary to the clear teaching of Scripture, Catholic theology also suggests the border between Hades and paradise is porous. The concept of purgatory is a Catholic doctrine of the afterlife that developed from a passage found in an apocryphal book called Second Maccabees, not included in the canon of Scripture recognized by Protestants. By definition, purgatory is a temporary place of suffering where the final purification of those destined for heaven happens. Catholic scholars believe this purification must take place because some people lack the holiness necessary to enter heaven. Purgatory runs contrary to the Reformers' idea of imputed righteousness; it also weakens the sufficiency of the cross of Christ to fully redeem us by grace and through faith alone.

Purgatory gained popularity during the Medieval period. At that same time in church history, Catholic leaders tied their fundraising to purgatory. Indulgences were spiritual favors offered by priests in return for a financial contribution to the church. For example, priests would pray for dead loved ones suffering in purgatory by promising parishioners, "As soon as the coin in the coffer rings, the soul in purgatory springs."[13] Pope Leo X actually funded the building of Saint Peter's Basilica in Rome by selling indulgences. However, clever slogans and good marketing never make up for bad theology.

DID JESUS GO TO HELL?

Some people wonder, "Did Jesus go to hell between His death and resurrection?" A close look at Scripture reveals no, not exactly. But according to Ephesians 4:8-9 and 1 Peter 3:18-20, His spirit descended into the "lower regions of the earth," presumably the paradise compartment of Hades. This is why He said to the thief on the cross, "Today, you will be with me in Paradise" (Luke 23:43).

Now here's where it gets a bit tricky to follow as things related to the afterlife begin to shift in the New Testament. If you haven't already done so, read the aforementioned passages carefully and in several translations. Also, stop by Revelation 1:18 where Jesus says He holds the keys of Death and Hades in His hand.

Are you with me so far?

Jesus went to Hades not hell and "proclaimed to the spirits in prison." The word translated "proclaimed" is the Greek word *kerysso*, which means "to preach." Yes, Jesus preached a sermon in Hades. What did He preach? We don't have a record of His sermon, but it's reasonable to assume that He proclaimed "liberty to those who are oppressed" (Luke 4:18 NASB). We know Jesus rose from the dead and later ascended to the Father as recorded in Acts 1. At that time, He seized the keys of Death and Hades. Later in the progress of New Testament revelation, we learn from both Paul's and Peter's writings that, while in Hades, Jesus took the righteous dead with Him to heaven to be with the Father. Otherwise, why did He travel there?

My best understanding of Scripture is that paradise or Abraham's bosom is not technically heaven any more than Hades is hell. The relocation of the righteous dead includes all Old Testament saints and the thief on the cross, leaving Hades with a single compartment where the unrighteous dead experience unimaginable torment until the Great White Throne Judgment when they are raised and cast into the lake of fire forever (Revelation 20).

But, you ask, what about the apostle Paul who says he was "caught up into paradise" (2 Corinthians 12:3)? Is Paul talking about heaven when he mentions paradise? The answer is yes because by then Jesus had relocated paradise and its inhabitants to heaven.

Are you still with me? And so, when the apostle Paul writes the following words to the Corinthians, he is correct in a post-ascension kind of way by saying dead believers are "absent from the body" and "at home with the Lord."

> Therefore, being always of good courage, and knowing that while we are at home in the body we are absent from the Lord—for we walk by faith, not by sight—we are of good courage, I say, and prefer rather to be absent from the body and to be at home with the Lord (2 Corinthians 5:6-8 NASB).

That's a long way around the block to say this: today, the hope of every believer in Jesus Christ is that sixty seconds after we die, we are absent from the body and forever present with the Lord in heaven. I call that good news! The unrighteous dead are likewise absent from the body but experiencing torment in Hades. Paul goes on to sober up believers with these words:

> So whether we are at home or away, we make it our aim to please him. For we must all appear before the judgment seat of Christ, so that each one may receive what is due for what he has done in the body, whether good or evil (2 Corinthians 5:9-10).

As believers who follow hard after Jesus, we must seize every precious moment in this life with the understanding there's no second chance, not even to earn rewards in heaven. Sixty seconds after we die, our experience in heaven will in some measure be a reflection of how well we pleased the Lord on earth, as revealed at the Judgment Seat of Christ, a future event in Bible prophecy we will discuss in full in a later chapter.

8

Can We Communicate with the Dead?

Hollywood has enjoyed a lengthy love affair with the occult. Not long ago, television shows like *Bewitched* and *Sabrina the Teenage Witch* were both huge hits. They featured psychic characters that appeared as everyday mortals like you and me but with special powers. *Ghost Whisperer* starring Jennifer Love Hewitt was another popular Hollywood drama. Hewitt played Melinda, who lived in the fictional town of Grandview, New York. She sees and talks to the dead. You read that right. She's a necromancer. The co-executive producer of the program was James Van Praagh, known as "television's most famous medium."

At the age of fourteen, Van Praagh entered a preseminary to become a Catholic priest. While there, he says he heard voices that told him "God is much bigger than these four walls; you must leave and find God outside in the world." At that moment, his interest in organized religion ended and his journey toward spirituality began. According to his website, he now dedicates his life to "changing the consciousness of the planet." Through his Center for Spiritual Living, Van Praagh claims to "bridge the gap between two planes of existence, that of the living and that of the dead by providing evidential proof of life after death via detailed messages."[14]

So, what are we to think of people like James Van Praagh or John Edward of *Crossing Over* fame? Can they really bridge the living and the dead, or are they merely clever marketers of false spirituality? And what about Hollywood's affection for the occult? Is it mere entertainment or something darker and more sinister? I'm old enough to remember when singer and songwriter Dionne Warwick hosted infomercials on the popular Psychic Friends Network. Are psychics our friends or modern-day scam artists? Yes, we've come a long way since *I Dream of Jeannie.*

Any discussion about death and the afterlife leads to questions about communicating with the dead. *Can* we communicate with the dead? And if we can, should we? Are the dead trying to communicate with us? And if they are, should we listen? The Bible is always the best place to form any theology about the afterlife. So, let's open up its pages again and blow the dust off the book of Leviticus.

> "Do not turn to mediums or necromancers; do not seek them out, and so make yourselves unclean by them: I am the LORD your God" (Leviticus 19:31).
>
> "If a person turns to mediums and necromancers, whoring after them, I will set my face against that person and will cut him off from among his people" (Leviticus 20:6).
>
> "A man or a woman who is a medium or a necromancer shall surely be put to death. They shall be stoned with stones; their blood shall be upon them" (Leviticus 20:27).

Those are not easy words to digest. The Lord calls anyone "unclean" who dabbles in the dark world of mediums and necromancers. They "shall surely be put to death"! It shouldn't surprise us to find such dire warnings in the book of Leviticus. The third book of the Pentateuch is God's handbook on holiness.

Necromancy is the practice of talking to the spirits of dead people or using magic powers for evil purposes. Author J.K. Rowling introduced necromancy to a new generation of curious young people and their parents through her blockbuster "Harry Potter" book series, later turned into a movie franchise. Since the publication of *Harry Potter and the Sorcerer's Stone* in 1997, some estimate between 400 and 500 million copies have been sold in the seven-book collection. You can now even visit The Wizarding World of Harry Potter at the Universal Studios Florida theme park in Orlando. The special effects are quite enchanting and guaranteed to charm us into believing evil is really harmless.

Before the devil gets too excited about his publishing success, I want to remind him the Bible is still, and always will be, the bestselling book of all time and eternity (Isaiah 55:11). And besides, the God of the Bible has strong words for necromancers and for anyone who turns to wizards like Harry Potter or Theresa Caputo for counsel.

Who is Theresa Caputo? She is the popular *Long Island Medium* who appears weekly on The Learning Channel (TLC). The self-styled "all-around family gal" claims, "I've been seeing, feeling, and sensing Spirit since I was four years old, but it wasn't until I was in my 20s that I learned to communicate with souls in Heaven."[15] Caputo might be winsome, but the Lord says this about the necromancer, "I will set my face against that person and I will cut him off from among his people." Those are strong words that should be taken seriously in any generation. Today, we give Hollywood fame to wizards, witches, and necromancers; but we should never forget that in Moses's day the medium was put to death!

From Leviticus, let's go to the book of Deuteronomy. In the fifth book of the Pentateuch, Moses delivers a series of talks to a new generation of Israelites as they get ready to cross over the Jordan River and take possession of the Promised Land. Through the leader of the Israeli Exodus, the Lord warned His people about participating in the occult practices of the pagan nations that currently occupied the land.

> "When you come into the land that the LORD your God is giving you, you shall not learn to follow the abominable practices of those nations. There shall not be found among you anyone who burns his son or his daughter as an offering, anyone who practices divination or tells fortunes or interprets omens, or a sorcerer or a charmer or a medium

> or a necromancer or one who inquires of the dead, for whoever does these things is an abomination to the LORD. And because of these abominations the LORD your God is driving them out before you. You shall be blameless before the LORD your God, for these nations, which you are about to dispossess, listen to fortune-tellers and to diviners. But as for you, the LORD your God has not allowed you to do this" (Deuteronomy 18:9-14).

Again, the Lord pulls no punches by using the word "abomination" to describe anyone who practices the occult. Abomination refers to something vile, shameful, or detestable.

Why are such practices so repulsive to a holy God?

Divination comes from a Hebrew word that means "to divide." The one who practices divination gives a false prophecy that is meant to tear apart not unite. On the contrary, the prophetic revelation God gives through His word is always meant for our good. A sorcerer seeks to control people and circumstances by casting spells through the power of evil spirits. The person who "casts spells" is literally the "one who ties knots." In other words, the casting of spells produces spiritual bondage, not freedom. The "charmer," "medium," or "necromancer" supposedly communicates with the dead but actually dances with demons.

Interpreting omens is another common practice of people tied to the occult. This has to do with predicting the future based on signs in nature.[16] Caputo describes how she interprets signs:

> "Spirit also uses a vocabulary of signs and symbols that they show me during a reading; over time, I assigned words, phrases, and meanings to certain images I was shown, and then through trial and error, Spirit helped me add new ones until we created an entire vocabulary for us to work with. I translate my signs and what I feel as best I can, and then deliver the messages, but it's the client's job to interpret how the meaning is significant. It's like piecing together a puzzle, and can sometimes sound like guesswork,

> but Spirit speaks 'another language,' at another speed, and in another dimension."[17]

A loud alarm should sound in our spirit whenever we come near such things. Think about how the Lord feels when His people seek the advice of fortune-tellers. Imagine if your child decided to seek the counsel of a friend's parents while simultaneously rebelling against your advice. Your daughter's friend and her parents do not share your family's values. In fact, they take the polar opposite position on virtually everything related to the raising of your children in a Christian home. While they appear as nice people and even smile in your presence, they possess an unmistakable agenda to lead the children of this generation astray, and they are doing a good job of it with your daughter. If you are like Cathryn and me, you would come uncorked if something like that happened to your family. God feels the same way, even stronger, when His kids seek the counsel of demons who are bent on destroying us. He even links rebellion to the sin of divination (1 Samuel 15:23). No matter how curious we are about the afterlife, the Lord's warnings about the occult are real and should be taken seriously.

For those reasons and more, I am greatly concerned about the pagan shrine recently erected on the campus of the United States Air Force Academy with the use of money from the U.S. taxpayer. It should cause every American great concern as it provides more evidence that we've become "one nation under many gods." According to an article published in the *Los Angeles Times,*

> "The Academy dedicated an $80,000 outdoor worship center—a small Stonehenge-like circle of boulders with propane fire pit—high on a hill for the handful of current or future cadets whose religion falls under the broad category of 'Earth-based.' Those include pagans, Wiccans, druids, witches and followers of Native American faiths."

What in America is going on? In the name of religious freedom, the United States government raised a pagan shrine at one of its prestigious military academies located in the beautiful Colorado mountains. Soon after, officials at West Point and Annapolis inquired about replicating the Air Force's efforts. I'm in favor of how the United States of America allows for and preserves religious liberty. However, I am also compelled to say the worship site for witches and warlocks at the U.S. Air Force Academy is still an abomination in God's eyes. If the Lord is true to His word, He will not allow this action to go unpunished.

Whether short-lived or lengthy, a curious love affair with the occult is never a good idea. King Saul learned this the hard way. Let's explore his attempt to communicate with the dead in the next chapter.

9

Saul and the Witch of Endor

No event in the Bible raises more questions about the occult and communicating with the dead than when King Saul consulted the witch of Endor. Even Hollywood knows the story. On the hit television show *Bewitched*, Agnes Moorehead played a witch named Endora, the antagonistic mother-in-law of Darrin Stephens, an ordinary mortal man. Her name comes from the twenty-eighth chapter of 1 Samuel where Saul visited a witch who lived in a place called Endor. Let's take a closer look beginning in verse 3.

> Now Samuel had died, and all Israel had mourned for him and buried him in Ramah, his own city. And Saul had put the mediums and the necromancers out of the land. The Philistines assembled and came and encamped at Shunem. And Saul gathered all Israel, and they encamped at Gilboa. When Saul saw the army of the Philistines, he was afraid, and his heart trembled greatly. And when Saul inquired of the Lord, the Lord did not answer him, either by dreams, or by Urim, or by prophets. Then Saul said to his servants, "Seek out for me a woman who is a medium that I may go to her and inquire of her." And his servants said to him, "Behold, there is a medium at En-dor" (1 Samuel 28:3-7).

Saul was Israel's first king. Against the Lord's better counsel, the people demanded a king like all the other nations. Eventually the Lord relented and gave them Saul. Not a man after God's own heart, as was David, his successor, Saul is a pathetic figure in the Bible. When God stripped the kingdom from Saul's hands and gave it to David, Saul became bitter and jealous. It didn't help when David's popularity rose like a rocket and the wooing women made comparisons of the two by singing, "Saul has slain his thousands, and David his ten thousands" (1 Samuel 18:7 NASB).

When Saul became king, he banned occult practices and tore down the pagan shrines just as the Lord told him to do. Three cheers for Saul! At least he started in the right direction. However, he left the backdoor of his heart open to demons. One day, fear gripped the king as the army of the Philistines gathered against Israel. When the Lord did not speak to him through the usual means (prayer, dreams, Urim, and prophets), Saul took matters into his own hands. He made a move to the dark side by seeking the counsel of a fortuneteller. Let's read on.

> So Saul disguised himself and put on other garments and went, he and two men with him. And they came to the woman by night. And he said, "Divine for me by a spirit and bring up for me whomever I shall name to you." The woman said to him, "Surely you know what Saul has done, how he has cut off the mediums and the necromancers from the land. Why then are you laying a trap for my life to bring about my death?" But Saul swore to her by the LORD, "As the LORD lives, no punishment shall come upon you for this thing" (1 Samuel 28:8-10).

Saul disguised himself and stepped boldly into the shadowy world of evil spirits. It's no accident that he "came to the woman by night" because anyone who operates in the demonic world walks in spiritual darkness. The fortuneteller had her guard up and didn't want to fall into a death trap. In a strange turnabout, Saul swore by the Lord's name that no harm would come to her.

"Then the woman said, 'Whom shall I bring up for you?' He said,

'Bring up Samuel for me'" (1 Samuel 28:11). What a strange request! There's no record of Saul ever seeking Samuel's advice when he was alive. So why would he do so from the deceased prophet of God? There's only one answer: Saul was a desperate man. It was typical of him to use religion and false spirituality as a convenient means to one of his selfish ends. Perhaps this is why the Lord turned a deaf ear to Saul's repeated inquiries.

Before the woman could say hocus-pocus, Samuel appeared, startling her so much that she cried out with a loud voice. Her surprise leads me to believe Samuel's appearance had nothing to do with her powers as a medium. Necromancers never actually communicate with the dead; rather, they see and talk to demons who pose as dead friends and relatives. Remember, the devil and his demons are masters of deception, appearing as angels of light (2 Corinthians 11:14). However, in this rare case, God allowed Samuel's spirit to appear and speak to Saul from the realm of the dead. Samuel was not the least bit happy about being disturbed. Let's read on in verse 15.

> Then Samuel said to Saul, "Why have you disturbed me by bringing me up?" Saul answered, "I am in great distress, for the Philistines are warring against me, and God has turned away from me and answers me no more, either by prophets or by dreams. Therefore I have summoned you to tell me what I shall do." And Samuel said, "Why then do you ask me, since the LORD has turned from you and become your enemy? The LORD has done to you as he spoke by me, for the LORD has torn the kingdom out of your hand and given it to your neighbor, David. Because you did not obey the voice of the LORD and did not carry out his fierce wrath against Amalek, therefore the LORD has done this thing to you this day. Moreover, the LORD will give Israel also with you into the hand of the Philistines, and tomorrow you and your sons shall be with me. The LORD will give the army of Israel also into the hand of the Philistines." Then Saul fell at once full length on the ground, filled with fear because of the words of Samuel (1 Samuel 28:15-20).

"The LORD has turned from you and become your enemy." Ouch! Saul couldn't have heard worse news from Samuel. Upon hearing the kingdom now belonged to David, fear filled Saul's heart. Furthermore, not only would the Philistines defeat Israel, but Samuel predicted Saul's own death and the death of his sons. And that's exactly what happened the very next day.

Saul's life reads like a Shakespearean tragedy. He had everything going for him. He came from a wealthy and influential family. It didn't hurt that his tall, handsome frame gave him a commanding presence when he walked into a room. As Israel's first king, the Spirit of the Lord came mightily upon him, giving him early success over his enemies. However, Saul was full of pride and obeyed the Lord selectively. No wonder the Lord stopped listening to his prayers and tore the kingdom from his hands. There's much we can learn from Saul's journey to the dark side.

LESSONS LEARNED FROM SAUL'S JOURNEY TO THE DARK SIDE

The first lesson we learn from Saul's journey to the dark side is the Lord's silence does not give us permission to explore the occult for answers about the afterlife. As I mentioned previously, Saul sought the Lord's counsel through all the usual means including something called the Urim. The Urim and Thummim were stones in the high priest's breastplate (Exodus 28:30 and Numbers 27:21). It's unclear in Scripture exactly how they were used to discern God's will, but not even the Urim yielded the answers Saul wanted to his questions. That's when he decided to dance with demons.

God is more than willing to communicate His will to us today. However, His primary means of doing so is through His Word and the indwelling Holy Spirit. He also uses the wise, biblical counsel of friends. He uses circumstances to lead us too. However, as believers we can shut down all communication with God by grieving, quenching, or resisting the Holy Spirit. And, our prayers lift no higher than the ceiling in our bedroom if we walk in disobedience to the Lord's commands as

Saul did. Psalm 66:18 (NASB) says, "If I regard wickedness in my heart, the Lord will not hear."

Second, practitioners of the occult have Satan and his demons as sources of information. I have already alluded to the fact that when mediums say they are talking to your dead loved one, they are most likely communicating with or through a demon posing as the deceased. Of course, some practitioners of the occult are merely showmen and tricksters. But it is completely within the realm of Scripture to conjure the spirit world. And remember, the Bible says, "For even Satan disguises himself as an angel of light. So it is no surprise if his servants, also, disguise themselves as servants of righteousness" (2 Corinthians 11:14-15).

Finally, beware of the occult disguised as entertainment. Books, movies, television shows, and video games with occult themes can appear harmless enough. However, they can also become gateways to a dark world. In which case I say *believer beware*! Even seemingly harmless games like the popular Ouija board introduce players to the occult in ways that can be dangerous. Flee such things. Stay far away from them. Dabbling in the occult will always leave you deceived and disillusioned. That's why the Bible discourages us from doing so in the strongest terms possible.

For example, Isaiah 8:19 says, "And when they say to you, 'Inquire of the mediums and the necromancers who chirp and mutter,' should not a people inquire of their God? Should they inquire of the dead on behalf of the living?"

Can we communicate with the dead? The better question is *should we*? The obvious answer is no!

10

Are You a Citizen of Heaven?

"How far would you travel to find a better life?" That's the question you'll read on the Ellis Island home page. The website goes on to introduce the historic site managed by the National Park Service by saying, "If you answered 'Whatever it takes,' you echo the feelings of 12 million immigrants who passed through these now quiet halls from 1892 to 1954." Ellis Island—a place of hope for some and tears for others—is the location in New York Harbor near the Statue of Liberty where millions of people from around the globe began their quest for the American dream.

Immigration policy has always been a hot political topic, and never more so than today. We can all agree on one thing: America is a nation of immigrants. Either we or our ancestors came to the United States from a country near or far away. The goal of every immigrant is to become a citizen. The one thing all citizens have in common is our love for freedom and the place where liberty finds exceptional expression in the greatest nation on earth. Anyone who has gone through the long and arduous process of becoming a legal U.S. citizen speaks with an appropriate measure of pride when he or she says, "I am an American!"

For good reasons, no country on earth has more people wanting to immigrate than the United States of America.

As much as I love my country, I must also remember that I possess a dual citizenship and a singular loyalty as a follower of Jesus Christ. Consider the apostle Paul's words to the Philippians, "But our citizenship is in heaven, and from it we await a Savior, the Lord Jesus Christ, who will transform our lowly body to be like his glorious body, by the power that enables him even to subject all things to himself" (Philippians 3:20-21).

Perhaps like you, I am a native-born citizen of the United States of America. Born in the USA and proud of it! However, I am first a citizen of heaven, a status that was granted to me when I was "born again" through faith in the Lord Jesus Christ (John 3:6). Unlike the process immigrants must go through to become legal citizens of the United States, I didn't earn my heavenly citizenship, and neither did you. Nor did it cost us any money. Jesus paid it all on the old rugged cross. We are citizens of heaven by God's amazing grace.

The Philippians too were proud Roman citizens, but Paul reminds them of their heavenly citizenship and the loyalty expected by it. As Bible teacher Warren Wiersbe notes, "Just as Philippi was a colony of Rome on foreign soil, so the church is a 'colony of heaven' on earth."[18] As members of heaven's earthly colony, we await our Savior's return. Our hope is rooted in the same power that raised Jesus from the dead.

A small percentage of people were denied entry into America at Ellis Island. That's why it was an Isle of Tears for some. The diseased and derelicts were disallowed from entering the country. Some might have lacked the education or a trade skill that would have contributed to making our country strong. Our borders have always been open to law-abiding people who possess certain qualities that make America a better place. However, not one of us is qualified to make heaven a better place. At the risk of sounding like a broken record, we are sinners saved by God's grace and through simple faith in the Lord Jesus, and that is the only way we become citizens of heaven. Unlike the tired, the poor, and the huddled masses that came to Ellis Island, the Bible says this about those who lay claim to a heavenly citizenship:

> For consider your calling, brothers: not many of you were wise according to worldly standards, not many were powerful, not many were of noble birth. But God chose what is foolish in the world to shame the wise; God chose what is weak in the world to shame the strong; God chose what is low and despised in the world, even things that are not, to bring to nothing things that are, so that no human being might boast in the presence of God (1 Corinthians 1:26-29).

If you think you have something to offer heaven, think again! God chooses foolish, weak, lowly, and despised people. The Almighty finds useful those that the world casts aside as useless. To that point, Jesus said the kingdom of heaven belongs to those who admit they are spiritually bankrupt (Matthew 5:3). Are you "yearning to breathe free"? Think of the cross as a statue of liberty for spiritual immigrants "who once were far off [but] have been brought near by the blood of Jesus Christ" (Ephesians 2:13).

The Bible also says believers in Jesus are seated right now with Him in the heavenly places, a reference to unseen spiritual realities (Ephesians 2:4-7). This is true even though I haven't actually visited the place where I will live for eternity. Furthermore, my real home is not 1250 Cherry Blossom Drive (nor is it my real address) because, as the apostle Peter notes, Christians are "strangers and pilgrims" in this world (1 Peter 2:11 KJV).

Living in this fallen, unfinished world is sort of like traveling in a foreign country. I always enjoy the trip but it never feels like home. My bags are packed for heaven and my eternal passport is stamped in the color red with the blood of Jesus Christ. All of that means I'm just passing through this world and so are you. That's why we should never get too comfortable on planet Earth or anxious about what happens here during our brief sojourn. The Bible says, "Set your affection on things above, not on things on the earth" (Colossians 3:2 KJV).

That said, heavenly minded with no earthly good is no way to live, but the opposite extreme is no good either. Some Christians I know are so earthly-minded that they never give their eternal home a second thought. In contrast, consider what the writer of Hebrews says about the way Abraham lived:

> By faith he went to live in the land of promise, as in a foreign land, living in tents with Isaac and Jacob, heirs with him of the same promise. For he was looking forward to the city that has foundations, whose designer and builder is God (Hebrews 11:9-10).

Abraham lived by faith, "as in a foreign land" and "in tents." Somebody once pointed out to me that Abraham always pitched his tents and built his altars. Intrigued, I read his story in the Old Testament again and found that to be true. The aged patriarch and friend of God never does the reverse, build his tents and pitch his altars. Not once. Knowing that the Bible is written by inspiration of the Holy Spirit and the third member of the Holy Trinity never wastes words, I knew this order and repetition pointed to something significant (2 Timothy 3:16).

Abraham lived with a keen understanding of the temporal and eternal. On earth he kept his tent pegs short because he knew this life is momentary and fleeting. No doubt, this made it easier for him to yank up his tents at age seventy-five, leave a comfortable retirement in the Ur of Chaldees (modern Iraq) with his wife Sarah, and join God on a new adventure. Along the way, Abraham built his altars to last because eternal things mattered most to him. He truly lived as a citizen of the city whose builder and maker is God.

As a pastor and radio broadcaster, I have the privilege of interacting with a number of Christian business people who remind me of Abraham. They take big, faith-filled risks every day in various segments of our economy. And when the profits come rolling in, they first set their affections on things above. Before they buy a new car or update their vacation home, they build an altar to God that lasts. They think, act, and invest their money like citizens of heaven first. The way they use their profits to invest in eternal things is truly inspiring.

More often than not we invest in the things we believe in. For example, "Buy American" is a popular slogan in the United States for patriotic citizens who want to support the U.S. economy. Many of us also look for a "Made in the U.S.A." label when making purchases. It connects with our sense of loyal citizenship. Heaven-bound believers in Jesus Christ should also embrace their true citizenship by investing accordingly but for entirely different reasons. That brings me to something else the Bible tells us about heaven. Our treasures are stored there.

Treasures in Heaven

I have always loved Jesus's practical, kingdom-focused teaching in what's known as His Sermon on the Mount. Smack in the middle of Matthew 5–7, he turns our attention to such mundane matters as where we invest our money. That's because our spiritual life and our financial life are intertwined. So, strap on your money belt and read these thought-provoking words slowly and carefully, and be prepared for them to rattle your investment cage.

> Do not lay up for yourselves treasures on earth, where moth and rust destroy and where thieves break in and steal; but lay up for yourselves treasures in heaven, where neither moth nor rust destroys and where thieves do not break in and steal. For where your treasure is, there your heart will be also (Matthew 6:19-21).

Everyone I know is looking for a good investment tip. Wouldn't you like to sink your money into the next Microsoft or Dell before the price of the stock rises like a rocket into the equities stratosphere? And wouldn't you like to know that your investment is safe from the whimsical ups and downs of the market, sometimes driven by political shenanigans in Washington and elsewhere in the world? Okay, then listen to what Jesus says: pull everything out of earth and put it into heaven. That's what I call a radical investment plan.

Can you imagine Jesus appearing as a guest on the Fox Business Network with Neil Cavuto and offering this kind of investment advice? The self-proclaimed Wall Street gurus would yield a collective gasp before laughing Him off the program. However, Jesus has an eternal perspective not often found in high-flying investment circles. He simply divides our thinking into two portfolios. One is earthly and the other is eternal.

Think of it this way. We build an earthly investment portfolio by receiving interest, dividends, and capital gains. Buying low and selling high is the way to increase our wealth on earth. Our risk tolerance must be taken into consideration too. An eternal portfolio, on the other hand, grows by giving some or all of our money away to fund kingdom causes. Our risk tolerance (also known as faith) must also be considered. Because it's more blessed to give than to receive (Acts 20:35), and because heavenly returns are protected and guaranteed, it's better to store up our treasures in heaven rather than on earth. Besides, the old adage is true: we can't take it with us, but we can surely send it ahead. So, what's in your wallet or safe? Maybe a better question is how much treasure do you have stored in heaven?

Jesus has a vision for your financial life that is truly out of this world. To say that believers in Jesus Christ have a heavenly 401(k) account is pretty close to the truth. The apostle Paul refers to this account in his letter to the Philippians. As he spoke to them about supporting his ministry financially, he writes, "Not that I desire your gifts. What I desire is that more be credited to your account" (Philippians 4:17 NIV).

Paul didn't want something *from* the Philippians; he wanted something *for* them. That's also what Jesus has in mind when He says, "But store up *for yourselves* treasures in heaven." I call this "sanctified self-interest" and believe it suggests there are certain benefits attached to the eternal investments we make, benefits we'll enjoy when we get to heaven. Larry Burkett of Crown Financial Ministries used to say, "The Lord tells us that there is really something akin to the First National Bank of Heaven, and He wants us to know that we can invest for eternity." The good news is the First National Bank of Heaven will never need a government bailout!

If the *Wall Street Journal* is correct, most people fail to plan financially on earth. Bankrate.com estimates that 76 percent of Americans live paycheck to paycheck.[19] That's scary to think about for a financially planned guy like me. I have a sneaky feeling that many Christians have also failed to lay up for themselves treasures in heaven, which is equally disconcerting for me as a pastor. Studies consistently show that the average churchgoing person gives no more to kingdom causes than the average pagan does to charity (around 2.5 percent of income). That means most Christians are leaving their heavenly 401(k) terribly underfunded.

If we dare to think about it, the implications of Jesus's teaching are staggering. For example, I believe heaven will be heavenly for every person who is there by faith in the Lord Jesus Christ. But heaven will be *more heavenly* for those who store up eternal treasures for themselves by investing their money in the Lord's gospel work while on earth. I'm not at all suggesting we can buy our way into heaven. No. Never. However, rewards in heaven will be based on how we worked out our salvation on earth, and that has stewardship implications related to the money God has entrusted to us (Ephesians 2:8-10; Philippians 2:12).

For the heaven-bound believer in Jesus Christ, generous giving is truly the smartest and safest way to invest your money because you can never lose what you put into your eternal portfolio. And the returns are truly heavenly! Thieves will not steal it, rust cannot corrode it, and moths cannot eat it. Furthermore, inflation cannot rob your eternal investment of its purchasing power. Seminary professor, author, and radio Bible teacher Haddon Robinson agrees when he writes,

> Two thousand years have passed. The situation may have changed but the reality hasn't. Stocks and bonds are at the mercy of a changing market. Inflation, like a rat, can nibble away at a bank account. Currency can be devalued. Houses, boats, and cars are subject to fire, tornados, and rust. Even land can lose its value with just one chemical spill. Wherever we put our wealth, there are no guarantees. Only shortsighted investors build up portfolios on this earth. Jesus gave better advice on investments. Equities built up in heaven are more secure and bring better dividends.[20]

So, are you a citizen of heaven? One proof may be that your treasures are stored there.

11

Is Your Name Written in Heaven?

After this the Lord appointed seventy-two others and sent them on ahead of him, two by two, into every town and place where he himself was about to go. And he said to them, "The harvest is plentiful, but the laborers are few. Therefore pray earnestly to the Lord of the harvest to send out laborers into his harvest. Go your way; behold, I am sending you out as lambs in the midst of wolves. Carry no moneybag, no knapsack, no sandals, and greet no one on the road. Whatever house you enter, first say, 'Peace be to this house!' And if a son of peace is there, your peace will rest upon him. But if not, it will return to you. And remain in the same house, eating and drinking what they provide, for the laborer deserves his wages. Do not go from house to house. Whenever you enter a town and they receive you, eat what is set before you. Heal the sick in it and say to them, 'The kingdom of God has come near to you.' But whenever you enter a town and they do not receive you, go into its streets and say, 'Even the dust of your town that clings to our feet we wipe off against you. Nevertheless know this, that the kingdom of God has come near.' I tell you, it will be more bearable on that day for Sodom than for that town" (Luke 10:1-12).

I want you to try and picture in your mind what it was like for the disciples who participated in this ministry excursion.

Jesus sent out the seventy-two like an advance team that travels ahead of the president of the United States to prepare his visit. He pulled no punches by saying, "I am sending you out as lambs in the midst of wolves." Think about a Republican president sending his team into an area that votes primarily for Democrats and vice versa. Politics can be vicious; so can ministry. Furthermore, Jesus told them to leave their money, luggage, and sandals at home. Unlike American Express, Jesus's motto was "you'd better leave home without it." He also told them not to greet anyone along the way. Travel light and stay focused on the mission was the idea.

As the pairs of Christ followers journeyed from town to town, their message was simply, "The kingdom of God has come near to you." If a town rejected the arrival of the kingdom, Jesus told them to wipe the dust off their feet. "I tell you, it will be more bearable on that day for Sodom than for that town." Tough words. "That day" refers to a future time of divine judgment.

Jesus prepared His followers for the worst possible experience, but they came back high-fiving each other. Their genuine exhilaration could not be contained. Full of joy, they no doubt swapped stories of transformed lives, powerful healings, and the wow factor that even "the demons are subject to us in your name." They were successful, and yet they gave glory to God by ascribing their success to the power of Jesus's holy name. That's when Jesus brought them back down to earth with these words,

> And he said to them, "I saw Satan fall like lightning from heaven. Behold, I have given you authority to tread on serpents and scorpions, and over all the power of the enemy, and nothing shall hurt you. Nevertheless, do not rejoice in this, that the spirits are subject to you, but rejoice that your names are written in heaven" (Luke 10:18-20).

Jesus saw the victories reported by the disciples as part of a spiritual conflict in the heavenly realms that defeated Satan, the serpent of old, and tossed him out of heaven along with his demons (Isaiah 14:4-23; Revelation 12:8-9). These were indeed great victories, as are all spiritual conquests, no matter how small they seem in our eyes. However, Jesus wanted the seventy-two to understand that the greatest miracle of all is still the salvation of a lost soul. "Nevertheless, do not rejoice in this, that the spirits are subject to you, but rejoice that your names are written in heaven," He says.

Our names are written in heaven? How and why? One Bible scholar notes,

> The Greek word translated "written" means "to inscribe formally and solemnly." It was used for the signing of a will, a marriage document, or a peace treaty, and also for the enrolling of a citizen. The perfect tense in the Greek means "it stands written."[21]

The best analogy is a guaranteed hotel reservation. In the hospitality industry, a reservation is guaranteed when the guest supplies the hotel with payment ahead of arrival, usually in the form of a credit card, cashier's check, or cash up front. This means a room will be held available for the guest regardless of the time he or she arrives. What does this have to do with our salvation? Jesus's death upon the cross and His shed blood guarantees our reservation in heaven when coupled with faith. This is the idea behind some of the last words Jesus uttered from the cross.

The Greek word *tetelestai* (translated "it is finished" in John 19:30) has various meanings but was commonly used in the first century by merchants who marked an invoice "paid in full." When Jesus used the word from the cross, it echoed through the halls of hell, signaling to a surprised devil that he had lost the cosmic battle between good and evil. The work was done. The price was paid in full. The Father's plan succeeded. All that remained was a victory party three days later. Now when a single soul expresses faith in the Lord Jesus Christ, the angels rejoice because a name is written down in the Lamb's book of life.

So why does our name need to be recorded in heaven? The last book of the Bible known as the Apocalypse of Jesus Christ gives us these sobering reasons,

> And if anyone's name was not found written in the book of life, he was thrown into the lake of fire (Revelation 20:15).
>
> But nothing unclean will ever enter it, nor anyone who does what is detestable or false, but only those who are written in the Lamb's book of life (Revelation 21:27).

At the end of time, God will scan heaven's records to see if your name and mine are recorded in the book of life. If they are, He will grant us entrance into His heavenly home. If not, a place more terrible than we can imagine awaits us.

Not long ago the Jones family was traveling on a summer vacation. We had a reservation to stay one night in a hotel in one of our favorite Southern cities, Charleston, South Carolina. We arrived and while checking in to the hotel, I knew something was amiss when the clerk took longer than usual to get the paperwork ready. She kept staring at the computer screen…and staring…and staring. That's when she said words that caused my heart to skip a beat, "Mr. Jones, your reservation is for tomorrow night." We had driven eight long hours to get there. I wasn't in any mood to go searching for another place to stay, nor was my weary family. I breathed a sigh of relief when she said the hotel still had vacancies for that night and she could change the reservation. I was given a second chance, but there are no second chances in the afterlife.

On another day, I was traveling with my son on a college visit to Chicago. We flew into Chicago O'Hare International Airport and then boarded a shuttle bus to pick up a rental car. We had a guaranteed reservation with Thrifty Car Rental, so I walked into the rental office and saw two people behind the reservation desk. One person was already serving a customer, so I walked over to the other clerk. I gave him my name. He couldn't find my reservation. I then gave him my confirmation code. He still couldn't find my reservation. Now I was getting worried and a bit agitated. That's when my son told me I was standing in line for the wrong car rental company. This was not the Thrifty office. How stupid of me! We went to Thrifty and were quickly assigned our reserved car.

If you're thinking you don't want to travel with the Joneses any time soon, I completely understand. But the point of me telling you my embarrassing reservation stories is to urge you to make your reservation in heaven. Jesus guaranteed your place in heaven with His blood, but you have to call on Him by faith to get your name written in the reservation book. Romans 10:13 says, "Everyone who calls on the name of the Lord will be saved."

Don't make the mistake of making the wrong reservation by following a false religion, or by just assuming a room in God's house will be waiting for you in the afterlife. It would be more than tragic to stand in line at the pearly gates, give your name to Saint Peter, and for him to look at you and say, "I'm sorry. We find no reservation in your name. We can only accommodate you in a place that has no air conditioning."

I don't mean to make light of a serious matter. Your eternal destination is of great concern to me. That's why I urge you to secure your reservation in heaven right now by expressing your faith in Jesus Christ through a simple prayer.

> Lord Jesus, I'm sorry for the things I've done wrong in my life. I agree with You that my actions are sinful and break Your perfect commands. I ask Your forgiveness and now turn from everything which I know is wrong to live for You. Thank You for dying on the cross to set me free from the sins that entangle me and to give me eternal life. Please come into my life and be with me forever. Thank You Lord Jesus, Amen.

There's nothing magical about saying these words. The "sinner's prayer" is not an incarnation. But if this prayer truly expresses the desire of your heart, welcome to God's family! Rest assured you are now a child of God and a citizen of heaven (John 1:12). I encourage you to get connected to a Bible-believing church so you can grow in your relationship with God and with others who love Jesus. As you do, love His appearing and look forward to the day when you can check into your eternal home, made secure by the price of your Savior's blood.

PRACTICAL IMPLICATIONS ON EARTH

As important as it is to know you've secured your reservation in heaven and your name is recorded there, the practical implication of doing so is peace and harmony in our earthly relationships. The apostle Paul made this clear in his brief letter to the Philippians.

> I entreat Euodia and I entreat Syntyche to agree in the Lord. Yes, I ask you also, true companion, help these women, who have labored side by side with me in the gospel together with Clement and the rest of my fellow workers, whose names are in the book of life (Philippians 4:2-3).

It's not hard to understand what's going on here. Two women in the church at Philippi named Euodia and Syntyche were in the kind of snarl that created real tension in the church. You could feel it when you walked through the door for worship. This is the only time the Bible mentions these ladies by name. How sad that they are known only for not getting along.

Apparently these women were not peripheral to Paul's ministry. They served alongside him and the rest of the ministry team. And get this—their names were written in the book of life, something they had in common with Paul, Clement, and the other fellow workers. In other words, they were Christians! They just weren't acting like Christians. Why does Paul mention this? Because, plain and simple, to have your name recorded in heaven's reservation book comes with the responsibility to preserve unity and peace in the body of Christ while on earth.

Heaven is a peaceful place. No wars or rumors of wars exist there. Not between nations, angels, redeemed people, or the Holy Trinity. What's true of heaven, where our citizenship is registered as believers in Jesus, should also be true on earth, especially in the church. Jesus said, "Blessed are the peacemakers, for they shall be called sons of God" (Matthew 5:9). Are you a peacemaker or a troublemaker? The names Euodia and Syntyche spelled T-R-O-U-B-L-E with a capital T. As James, the half-brother of Jesus, writes, "These things should not be so, my brothers and sisters" (James 3:10 NET).

My plea to you beyond making sure your name is written in heaven's reservation book is to make peace, not war in the church. As a pastor for more than twenty years, I'm amazed by the skirmishes that arise among God's people. Today, rarely are divisions in the church over matters of theology and doctrine. They usually result from somebody who gets upset because his or her feelings got hurt.

Turf wars and other kinds of tussles should not be named among God's people who profess the name of Jesus, and whose names are written in the book of life. "If possible, so far as it depends on you, live peaceably with all," writes Paul to the Romans (12:18). Since Christians will live in harmony for all of eternity, we might as well start practicing on earth today.

12

The Father's Big House

If you had less than twenty-four hours to live, what would you say to the people you love? How would you say farewell? How real would you get with them? On the night before His crucifixion, Jesus shared authentic moments and warm conversation with His closest friends and followers. They enjoyed a Passover meal together in an undisclosed room located above someone's living quarters in Jerusalem. It was there in an upper room that Jesus expressed these following heartfelt words to His disciples,

> "Let not your hearts be troubled. Believe in God; believe also in me. In my Father's house are many rooms. If it were not so, would I have told you that I go to prepare a place for you? And if I go and prepare a place for you, I will come again and will take you to myself, that where I am you may be also. And you know the way to where I am going." Thomas said to him, "Lord, we do not know where you are going. How can we know the way?" Jesus said to him, "I am the way, and the truth, and the life. No one comes to the Father except through me" (John 14:1-6).

Filled with anxiety, the disciples sensed something ominous was about to take place. It was time to celebrate a holy festival in the holy city, but Jesus had already told them, "The Son of Man must suffer many things and be rejected by the elders and chief priests and scribes, and be killed, and on the third day be raised" (Luke 9:22).

That's enough to make anybody shake in his sandals, and that's why Jesus interjected these soothing words, "Let not your hearts be troubled." He comforted His friends with the promise of heaven and said five things specifically about their eternal home.

Heaven Is a Real Place

There's no mistake in Jesus's mind that heaven is a real, physical place. Twice in John 14:1-6, he uses the Greek word *topos*, which is translated "place." For example, He says, "I go to prepare a place for you." In the ancient language, *topos* refers to a real, physical place. Furthermore, Jesus uses physical references like "rooms" and "house" to describe where the Father lives.

Revelation 21–22 describe heaven as a beautiful city in splendid detail. The holy city has walls, gates, foundations, streets, rivers, trees, vegetation, and more. While the Apocalypse of Jesus Christ is full of much symbolism, there is nothing in the context of those chapters that should lead us to believe heaven is anything other than a physical place.

All of that confirms that heaven is not the figment of a trumped-up religious imagination. Heaven is not Neverland or Candyland or Alice in Wonderland. Heaven is more than pie-in-the-sky-by-and-by. It's a real place where God the Father dwells and Jesus sits at His right hand. And if heaven is a real place, then so is hell. If hell is not a real place, then intellectual honesty demands that we say the same thing about heaven.

So, if heaven is a real place (and I believe it is), where exactly is it? The apostle Paul wrote about himself in the third person when he referred to a man who was "caught up into the third heaven... and he heard things that cannot be told, which man may not utter" (2 Corinthians 12:2-4). Some people believe this is a reference to an out-of-body or near-death experience when Paul was stoned and left for dead outside the city of Lystra (Acts 14). Paul says, "Whether in the body or out of the body I do not know, God knows." In this case, he enjoyed the freedom of saying "I don't know" and so should we about Paul's experience. But what does he mean by the "third heaven"? Is there a first and second heaven too?

In a departure from orthodox Christianity, Mormons believe there are multiple heavens. They teach about a Celestial Kingdom, a Terrestrial Kingdom, and a Telestial Kingdom. If you are good enough to obey all of God's law, you will live forever with Him in the third heaven or Celestial Kingdom. The other "kingdoms" are not as desirable, but they are still heaven. They are for people who tried hard to live a good life, but they didn't quite measure up to God's or Joseph Smith's standards.

Because Mormonism distorts orthodox Christianity in many more ways than this, and based on a careful study of Holy Scripture, I can only reject the Mormon view of multiple heavens and its good-works approach to getting there. Besides, there's a simpler explanation of the "third heaven" which Paul mentions in his letter to the Corinthians. Think of the first heaven as the sky and the earth's atmosphere. The second heaven is what we call outer space. The third heaven, where an omnipresent God dwells, is beyond all of that. A few verses later, Paul calls it paradise, the same place where Jesus said the thief on the cross would join Him.

Some scholars speculate that the place where God dwells could be another dimension that we cannot see with the naked eye. This makes some sense because God is spirit (John 4:24). After His resurrection and while in His glorified body, Jesus appeared to move in and out of a space-time dimension. For example, He traveled with two men on a road to Emmaus, but "their eyes were kept from recognizing him." When they drew near to the village, they shared a meal together. After Jesus blessed the food and broke bread, "their eyes were opened, and they recognized him. And he vanished from their sight" (Luke 24:31).

Poof! Jesus appeared and then disappeared. Where did He go? In the verses that follow in Luke's Gospel, He appears to the eleven in a way that startles them. Did He move through another space-time dimension? Earth to heaven and heaven to earth again? We don't know for sure. However, even if heaven is located in another dimension, it is no less real than the physical world we call earth. Jesus certainly thought of heaven as a real place.

HEAVEN IS A DIFFERENT PLACE THAN EARTH

I know you think I'm overstating the obvious by saying heaven is a different place than earth, but my point is this: heaven is not the good life we make for ourselves on earth. I often hear people, even some Christians, talk about their "little slice of heaven on earth." Usually, they're referring to a place they bought at the lake or a chateau they acquired in the mountains. If that describes you, I'm sorry to bust your bubble by saying *that's not heaven!* Not even close. Anyone's little slice of heaven on earth is a ghetto shack compared to the home Jesus is preparing for His followers. Besides, heaven is not earth and the old earth is certainly not heaven.

Jesus said, "I go to prepare a place for you." The word "go" implies He is leaving this earth for a different place. That's why the disciples were so upset. They didn't understand all that was happening, but they knew Jesus was soon departing from this world. They didn't know where He was going, just that He was leaving them. And He promised to return one day to take them to another place with Him. That place called heaven should get us more excited than any beautiful place we might visit on God's earth.

It's easy to make this earth feel like home. We grow deep roots here. And a little prosperity can make us so comfortable here that we're in no hurry to leave this place. On the contrary, the apostle Paul was "hard pressed" between earth and heaven. He said to his friends in Philippi, "My desire is to depart and be with Christ, for that is far better. But to remain in the flesh is more necessary on your account" (Philippians 1:23-24). God put a pulse for paradise in Paul's heart that made him yearn deeply for heaven. Does that pulse beat in your heart too, more than it does for any place on earth?

HEAVEN IS THE FATHER'S BIG HOUSE

Heaven is the place where God the Father dwells. We know that because Jesus taught us to pray, "Our Father who is in heaven" (Matthew 6 NASB).

To say that God dwells in heaven is not to place limitations on Him. The Bible teaches that God is omnipresent, meaning He is everywhere at all times (Psalm 139). But His primary and unique home is heaven.

Heaven is where God sits on His throne and makes the earth His footstool (Acts 7:49). As Ron Rhodes, author of *The Wonder of Heaven*, says, heaven is "the center of His providential operations throughout the universe, and the place where He is most perfectly worshiped by His creatures."[22] Heaven is also the Father's big, big house. How do we know that? Jesus said, "In my Father's house are many rooms." An older translation of the Bible says "many mansions," leading some to believe Jesus is building a mansion in the sky for them. For reasons I'll explain later, the better translation is "many rooms" or "many dwelling places."

Cathryn and I have friends in Dallas who live in a big house. Their house is so big it has a second-story dance studio where the wife teaches all kinds of dance moves to students and friends. They also have a slide that goes from the second floor to the first. Yes, a slide! We once held a ministry staff party there and after learning how to line dance, we all took a ride down the slide. It was a lot of fun!

But my friend's 6000-square-foot house is puny compared to the Father's big house. Exactly how big is God's house? How large is heaven? Revelation 21 describes the new heaven and the new earth God is preparing, and the new Jerusalem. Take a deep breath as you read this description of the future heaven:

> And I saw the holy city, new Jerusalem, coming down out of heaven from God, prepared as a bride adorned for her husband...And the one who spoke with me had a measuring rod of gold to measure the city and its gates and walls. The city lies foursquare, its length the same as its width. And he measured the city with his rod, 12,000 stadia. Its length and width and height are equal. He also measured its wall, 144 cubits by human measurement, which is also an angel's measurement (Revelation 21:2,15-17).

Even though the book of Revelation is filled with apocalyptic symbolism, there's every reason to understand these words literally. Some scholars see the heavenly city as a cube and others view it as a pyramid. Either way, as Ron Rhodes says,

> The heavenly city measures approximately 1500 miles by 1500 miles by 1500 miles...The eternal city is so huge that it would measure approximately the distance "from Canada to Mexico, and from the Atlantic Ocean to the Rockies." That is a surface area of 2.25 million square miles (by comparison, London is only 621 square miles)...The city is tall enough that from the earth's surface it would reach about one-twentieth of the way to the moon. If the city has stories, each being twelve feet high, then the city would have 600,000 stories. *That is huge!*[23]

There can only be one reason the future heavenly city is so big—to accommodate lots and lots of people! Throughout church history, this has led to speculation about how many redeemed people will live in heaven. Rhodes cites Norman Geisler, a scholar, who suggests the accumulative total of infants and children who died before the age of accountability must represent a large portion of the population of heaven. Geisler also points to, for example, the fifty million babies in America that never experienced life outside their mother's womb since the Supreme Court ruled in favor of abortion on demand. He believes every one of those aborted babies will add to heaven's population, making it the Father's big house.

Yes, Jesus said "only a few" will travel the road that leads to eternal life (Matthew 7). But that does not mean heaven will be sparsely populated. He means few compared to the many that go a different direction. Millions have come to the cross, and as the familiar song says, there's "Room at the Cross for You."

HEAVEN IS LIKE A WEDDING CELEBRATION

Let's go back to John 14 where Jesus said, "If I go and prepare a place for you, I will come again and receive you to Myself, that where I am, there you may be also" (v. 3 NJKV). Jesus had a first-century Middle Eastern wedding in mind when He spoke these words to His disciples. How so?

Weddings in Jesus's time were different from today's weddings in Western culture. For example, the groom was the center of attention in the first century, not the bride. Thus, at that time it made more sense to say "here comes the groom" than it did "here comes the bride." This is why the New Testament calls the church "the bride of Christ" and we eagerly await our heavenly Groom's return. It's all about Jesus, not us! The Second Coming of Jesus Christ is the "blessed hope" of the church (Ephesians 5:27; Titus 2:13).

Back then, the bride and groom also entered what's called a betrothal period which lasted for up to one year. It was like an engagement, only the couple was already legally married. However, no sexual relations were permitted. Mary and Joseph, Jesus's earthly parents, were betrothed to each other when Mary, a virgin, learned she was pregnant by the Holy Spirit.

It was customary during the betrothal for the groom to actually leave his bride and return to his father's house. He would spend the next twelve months or so adding rooms to his father's house because that's where he and his wife would live after their wedding. This is why I believe "many rooms" is a better translation in John 14:2 than "many mansions." Having said that, I still love to sing the old hymn "When We All Get to Heaven," especially the part that says, "In the mansions, bright and blessed, He'll prepare for us a place."

Are you starting to get the picture? Jesus used wedding imagery to comfort His disciples with the promise of heaven and the hope of His Second Coming. The disciples surely understood this. The wedding imagery carries over into the book of Revelation, which speaks of something called the "marriage supper of the Lamb." Revelation 19:6-9 reads,

> Then I heard what seemed to be the voice of a great multitude, like the roar of many waters and like the sound of mighty peals of thunder, crying out, "Hallelujah! For the Lord our God the Almighty reigns. Let us rejoice and exult and give him the glory, for the marriage of the Lamb has come, and his Bride has made herself ready; it was granted her to clothe herself with fine linen, bright and pure"—for

> the fine linen is the righteous deeds of the saints. And the angel said to me, "Write this: Blessed are those who are invited to the marriage supper of the Lamb." And he said to me, "These are the true words of God."

Do you have your wedding invitation? Everyone who places his or her faith in the Lord Jesus Christ is invited to the marriage supper of the Lamb. And make no mistake about it. Jesus won't leave His bride standing at the altar. He's coming back for His church as surely as the sun rises in the east and sets in the west.

The Way to Heaven Is Through Jesus

Who is Jesus? That's the question of the ages. Get the answer to that question right and everything else falls into place. And when Jesus answers the question in His own words, it becomes abundantly clear who the Nazarene really was. Are you among those who believe Jesus was merely a great man and a religious teacher who never claimed to be God? If yes, then consider one of His many acrimonious dealings with the Pharisees.

John's Gospel records a particularly heated exchange between Jesus and the Pharisees when they asked Him, "Are you greater than our father Abraham, who died?" Jesus replied to them, "Truly, truly, I say to you, before Abraham was, I am" (John 8:58). When the Jews heard Jesus say "I am," they believed He made Himself equal with God who said to Moses in the Old Testament, "This is what you are to say to the Israelites: 'I AM has sent me to you'" (Exodus 3:14 NIV). That's why they picked up stones to throw at Him.

John records in his Gospel seven self-revelatory statements Jesus made, each one claiming deity in a different way. They include, "I am the bread of life" (6:35), "I am the light of the world" (8:12), "I am the door" (10:9), "I am the good shepherd" (10:11), "I am the resurrection and the life" (11:25), "I am the true vine" (15:1), and "I am the way, and the truth, and the life" (14:6).

That's a long way around the block to point out that Jesus makes one of His last "I am" statements in the upper room with His disciples while conversing about heaven and His Second Coming. On the heels of it, He says, "No man comes to the Father except through me" (14:6). That's bold. No man means no man, woman, or child anywhere on earth or at any time in history. It's clear that Jesus saw Himself as the exclusive pathway to heaven.

The early church carried forward this idea. The apostle Peter refers to Jesus when he says, "And there is salvation in no one else, for there is no other name under heaven given among men by which we must be saved" (Acts 4:12).

Do you want to go to heaven when you die? You can only get there through Jesus. He has the right to make that claim because He died on the cross to pay the penalty for our sins. He then rose from the dead, defeating the last enemy and laying claim to His own words, "I am the resurrection and the life." Some people bristle at the idea that Jesus is the only way. But no other religious leader did what Jesus did, made the claims He made, or has His credentials. Jesus willingly died on the cross for our sins. In doing so, He made it possible for us to enjoy the Father's big house forever with Him.

13

Is Heaven for Real?

Heaven has always been the great anticipation of believers in Jesus Christ. No heaven, no hope. No afterlife, no purpose in this life. Even the prospect of judgment day is enough to make us think twice about how we live the one life God has given to us.

The apostle Paul was spot on when he said, "For now we see in a mirror dimly, but then face to face" (1 Corinthians 13:12). That's especially true as it relates to the afterlife. Scripture gives us fuzzy glimpses of the future eternal state. And even then, the writers, inspired as they were by the Holy Spirit, struggled to describe what they saw in visions and dreams.

Imagine traveling to a remote part of the world with a missionary and visiting a people group unreached by the gospel. They have lived for centuries in a dense region far, far away from what we would call civilization. They've never seen a big city with tall buildings that reach high into the sky. They can hardly imagine metro trains, buses, airplanes, and automobiles. Their mode of transportation is by foot or by paddling a canoe down the river. And so, how in the world would you explain megabytes, Wi-Fi, and smart phone technology to them?

Such is the struggle for those rare persons in Scripture that enjoyed a glimpse of heaven. The list is small—only four of them, including

Isaiah and Ezekiel in the Old Testament and the apostles Paul and John in the New Testament (Isaiah 6:1-4; Ezekiel 1:10; Revelation 4–6). We could stretch the list to six people by adding Micaiah and Stephen who both received peeks into the afterlife before going there (2 Chronicles 18:18; Acts 7:55). However, Scripture contains no detailed description of what these two men saw.

Taken together, author Phillip Johnson points out that "all of these were prophetic visions, not near-death experiences. Not one person raised from the dead in the Old or New Testaments ever recorded for us what he or she experienced in heaven. That includes Lazarus, who spent four days in the grave."[24]

This is important to remember in light of so many books and movies that tell fanciful stories of people who died, went to heaven, and came back to earth with eyewitness accounts of their afterlife experiences. The latest is a book by a Wesleyan pastor named Todd Burpo called *Heaven Is for Real.* More than seven million copies of the book were sold before televangelist and prosperity preacher T.D. Jakes produced the movie version.

Is heaven for real? The answer is yes, but not because Burpo's son, Colton, visited heaven at age four while in the hospital for an emergency appendectomy. Years later, Colton, now a teenager, has made some audacious claims. For example, he says while anesthetized he went to heaven and sat on Jesus's lap while the angels sang to him. He also got a halo and wings, although he says they were too small for him. He saw Mary, the mother of Jesus, standing next to the Almighty's throne and caught a view of the Holy Spirit who was "kind of blue." The boy also claims he saw his sister who had died in his mother's womb (something his parents never told him). The problem is that none of Colton Burpo's claims come close to what the Scripture says about the afterlife. And besides, the Bible is clear that when believers in Jesus go to heaven, we do not become angels with wings.

There's nothing new about the claims of people who say they nearly died and visited heaven. Burpo joins a long list of those who supplant the authority and sufficiency of Scripture with their own personal experiences. In the mid-1990s, New Age guru Betty Eadie released a book called *Embraced by the Light.* It quickly joined the *New York Times* bestseller list while boasting of "living proof that there is life after death."[25] Back then, most Christians possessed enough biblical discernment to see the publication for what it was—another false tale by a psychic trying to sell books about heaven. But today, biblical literacy is sadly at a low ebb and stories like Burpo's are easily embraced by the masses.

Eadie's book was originally published by Bantam Books under arrangement with Gold Leaf Press. However, a dramatic shift in publishing has taken place since then, noted by Phillip Johnson who says, "Peddling fiction about the afterlife as non-fiction is the current Next Big Thing in the world of evangelical publishing."[26] Millions of people who call themselves born-again Christians are buying the books and turning them into bestsellers. Some of the titles include *23 Minutes in Hell: One Man's Story About What He Saw, Heard, and Felt in that Place of Torment* by Bill Wiese, *The Boy Who Came Back from Heaven* by Kevin Malarkey, *90 Minutes in Heaven: A True Story of Death and Life* by Don Piper, and *Flight to Heaven: A Plane Crash… A Lone Survivor… A Journey to Heaven—and Back* by Dale Black. Most of it is malarkey—pure bunkum! Johnson goes on to say:

> Every week, I answer emails and inquiries from evangelicals who are confused by the barrage of afterlife travelogues. Why Christians who profess to believe the Bible would find these stories the least bit compelling is an utter mystery, but it is a sure sign that many in the evangelical movement have abandoned their evangelical convictions. Specifically, they have relinquished the principle of *sola Scriptura* and lost their confidence in the sufficiency of Scripture. Why else would they turn from clear biblical teaching on heaven and seek an alternative view in mystical experiences that bear no resemblance to what Scripture tells us?[27]

Why should we remain skeptical of near-death experiences? First, the term "near-death experience" invites suspicion all by itself. It's like saying a woman is nearly pregnant. Either you are, or you aren't.[28] Furthermore, the Bible makes it clear that nobody visits heaven after death and then returns to earth again. Agur, a small contributor to the book of Proverbs, asks, "Who has ascended to heaven and come down?" (Proverbs 30:4). Two thousand years later, Jesus answered that question by saying, "No one has ascended into heaven except he who descended from heaven, the Son of Man" (John 3:13). "No one" means *no one* except Jesus. Not Colton Burpo, Betty Eadie, Alex Malarkey, Don Piper, Dale Black, or anyone else who makes the misleading claim.

Besides, in the Bible, dead people don't take quick tours of heaven and then return to earth to write a book about it. At best, Scripture records the rare accounts of living people who saw heaven in a dream or vision and, like Paul, were reluctant to record their experience. The great apostle said he was "caught up to the third heaven...and he heard things that cannot be told, which man may not utter" (2 Corinthians 12:2-4). The phrases "cannot be told" and "may not utter" can refer to the fact that Paul was denied permission to speak. Or, perhaps they suggest the limits of his own language to describe the things he saw and experienced. Either way, Paul summarized his experience in a few verses not an entire book.

Another reason we should remain skeptical of near-death experiences is because Satan is a master of disguise and deception. The apostle Paul warned the Corinthians that sometimes the devil "disguises himself as an angel of light."

> For such men are false apostles, deceitful workmen, disguising themselves as apostles of Christ. And no wonder, for even Satan disguises himself as an angel of light. So it is no surprise if his servants, also, disguise themselves as servants of righteousness (2 Corinthians 11:13-15).

How ironic that many like Eadie who claim to have slipped into the afterlife report how they saw a bright light. It made them feel loved and welcomed. The light embraced them and told them everything would be okay. And they believed the light was divine. Are these stories true and reliable? Can we trust them to tell us what lies beyond the grave? The Bible leaves open the possibility that the enemy has fabricated near-death experiences in order to deceive many.

That said, in some cases I don't doubt the sincerity of those who report their near-death experience.

Author Robert Jeffress is the senior pastor of the historic First Baptist Church of Dallas, Texas, and has written a number of bestselling books. He has also appeared on most major media outlets like CNN, CNBC, and FOX News by offering an evangelical perspective on various cultural issues. In his book *How Can I Know? Answers to Life's 7 Most Important Questions* he points out, "Given the number of these experiences, they should not be completely dismissed." He goes on to say, "At the very least, these near-death experiences suggest that consciousness can survive the cessation of heart and brain activity for some undetermined period of time, suggesting there is some kind of existence that transcends physical life."[29]

Finally, skepticism abounds in my heart because the many reports of near-death experiences do not align with Scripture or even agree with each other. Isaiah's vision of heaven agrees perfectly with Ezekiel's as does Paul's with John's. There are no contradictions. However, none of the four biblical visions compare closely to Burpo's, Eadie's, or others. Johnson says, "Notably missing from all the biblical accounts are the frivolous features and juvenile attractions that seem to dominate every account of heaven currently on the bestseller lists."[30] Thus, we must make a decision: does the Bible or Burpo give us a more trustworthy account of the afterlife?

Recently, all of my skepticism was confirmed about people who supposedly died and went to heaven only to return with amazing tales. About one month before the manuscript for this book was due to my publisher, a story rocked the literary world and lingered for about 48 hours in the news cycle. The following headline by a blogger for the *Washington Post* said it all: "*Boy Who Came Back From Heaven* Actually Didn't; Books Recalled."[31]

The Boy Who Came Back from Heaven is the title of a bestselling book written in 2010 by Kevin Malarkey and his son, Alex Malarkey (yes, that's their real last name). It was published by Tyndale House Publishers and reportedly sold more than 1 million copies. Pitched as a "true story," the book chronicles what happened to Alex after a car accident left him in a coma for two months when he was six years old. He suffered debilitating paralysis and continues to struggle with his injuries today. Ron Charles calls the book "part of a popular genre of heavenly tourism." But Alex now confesses it was all a hoax. "I did not die. I did not go to heaven," the boy stated in an open letter. He also said,

> "Please forgive the brevity, but because of my limitations I have to keep this short…I said I went to heaven because I thought it would get me attention. When I made the claims that I did, I had never read the Bible. People have profited from lies, and continue to. They should read the Bible, which is enough. The Bible is the only source of truth. Anything written by man cannot be infallible."

Rewind. *They should read the Bible, which is enough.* That's what I've been saying all along, but Alex said it better and with fewer words. By now, you can easily guess where I stand. As for me and my house, the Bible is enough because it's the only reliable source of information about the afterlife.

In the pages of holy writ, God has already told us everything we need to know about the reality of heaven. If He thought we needed more information about life beyond the grave, don't you think Jesus would have held a press conference with Lazarus after He raised Him from the dead?

Heaven is for real because the Bible resoundingly declares its existence. Let's make sure we read God's love letter to us and learn all we can about our eternal home, while not falling prey to wild stories and silly speculations.

14

Heaven and the New Jerusalem

The Revelation of Jesus Christ is the last book of the Bible. It contains a thrilling ride through prophecy and end-time events on earth. It also concludes with the largest description of heaven and the eternal state found anywhere in Scripture. Would you like to take a closer look? Here's what the apostle John saw in a vision on the island of Patmos.

> Then I saw a new heaven and a new earth, for the first heaven and the first earth had passed away, and the sea was no more. And I saw the holy city, new Jerusalem, coming down out of heaven from God, prepared as a bride adorned for her husband. And I heard a loud voice from the throne saying, "Behold, the dwelling place of God is with man. He will dwell with them, and they will be his people, and God himself will be with them as their God. He will wipe away every tear from their eyes, and death shall be no more, neither shall there be mourning, nor crying, nor pain anymore, for the former things have passed away." And he who was seated on the throne said, "Behold, I am making all things new" (Revelation 21:1-5).

The first question that pops into my mind is why is God making all things new? I love new things as much as you do. I love the smell of a new car. I love a new home and my wife loves a new kitchen and new clothes. We love new beginnings and the rhythm of nature at the start of each new season. But why a new heaven and a new earth, and a new Jerusalem? What's wrong with the old heaven, the old earth, and the old Jerusalem?

It's easy to understand why God will make a new earth. Creation groans like Judge Roy Scream, an old and rickety wooden roller coaster I once rode at Six Flags Over Texas, which I'm embarrassed to admit made me scream like a six-year-old girl! This aging, fallen, and unfinished earth is stained and tarnished by sin, viciously marred by corruption. Despite the sincere efforts of some to save planet earth, its destruction is inevitable. It is worn out, winding down, and falling apart. After the cataclysmic days of the Tribulation period, a future event in Bible prophecy, humans will welcome a new earth. But why a new heaven and a new holy city?

At the very least, we can say God loves to create new things. God told Israel, "And I will give you a new heart, and a new spirit I will put within you" (Ezekiel 36:26). Paul writes to the Corinthians, "Therefore, if anyone is in Christ, he is a new creation. The old has passed away; behold, the new has come" (2 Corinthians 5:17). King David declared joyfully, "He put a new song in my mouth, a song of praise to our God" (Psalm 40:3). Thus, it shouldn't surprise us that God will make all things new again in the eternal state.

Of course this means the first earth and heaven must go away. John says, "I saw…the first heaven and the first earth had passed away." What does he mean by this and how will the present earth and heavens be destroyed? Peter gives us some insight in his second New Testament letter. False teachers scoffed at the idea of Jesus's soon return. That's when Peter wrote these words to encourage believers.

> They will say, "Where is the promise of his coming? For ever since the fathers fell asleep, all things are continuing as they were from the beginning of creation." For they deliberately overlook this fact, that the heavens existed long ago,

> and the earth was formed out of water and through water by the word of God, and that by means of these the world that then existed was deluged with water and perished. But by the same word the heavens and earth that now exist are stored up for fire, being kept until the day of judgment and destruction of the ungodly (2 Peter 3:4-7).

Peter reminds skeptics of the first time God brought destruction upon the earth. With the exception of Noah and his family, God destroyed all the inhabitants of the earth by a worldwide, cataclysmic flood. He then put a rainbow in the sky and said He would never do that again *by water.* But according to Peter, the next time God destroys the earth he will do so *by fire.*

Peter's use of the phrase "stored up for fire" has led some to speculate about the role of nuclear and atomic energy in the future destruction of the earth. Bible teacher Warren Wiersbe writes, "Modern atomic science has revealed that the elements that make up the world are stored with power. There is enough atomic energy in a glass of water to run a huge ocean liner. Man has discovered this great power and, as a result, the world seems to teeter on the brink of atomic destruction." Wiersbe goes on to say,

> However, Peter seems to indicate that *man* will not destroy the world by his sinful abuse of atomic energy. It is *God* who will "push the button" at the right time and burn up the old creation and all the works of sinful man with it; then He will usher in the new heavens and earth and reign in glory.[32]

Yes, there's a new world coming. Doesn't that sound exciting! The all-powerful God of the Bible will bring it into existence at a time of His choosing as He did the first heaven and earth. But that means the old world must first pass away to make room for the new.

Merging Heaven and Earth

It's important to make a distinction between heaven in the eternal state and heaven today, the place where departed spirits who believe in Jesus currently dwell. It appears from a careful reading of Revelation 21 that one day the new heaven and earth will exist as one continuous realm. It's hard to imagine, but the Bible pictures the new Jerusalem as "coming down out of heaven from God" to rest upon the new earth. In eternity, believers will exist in the new earth and heaven at the same time. Author Robert Jeffress points out,

> One of the greatest misconceptions about heaven is that it is located in some distant galaxy far, far away or in some invisible fourth dimension that will be inhabited by the disembodied spirits of Christians. Nothing could be further from the truth. The Bible teaches that the ultimate dwelling place for Christians will be a re-created earth, not an ethereal and undefined location in outer space.[33]

Jeffress makes perfect sense in light of what the Bible says about the righteous inheriting the earth (Psalm 37:9; Matthew 5:5). This re-created earth will also be the place where God lives with His people. The implications of verse 3 are heart throbbing:

> And I heard a loud voice from the throne saying, "Behold, the dwelling place of God is with man. He will dwell with them, and they will be his people, and God himself will be with them as their God" (Revelation 21:3).

Take a moment and let that sink in. The Bible begins with God creating the heavens and the earth, which included a special paradise called Eden where He dwelled with the humans He created in His own image. Before sin entered the world, God walked with Adam in the cool of the day and enjoyed conversations with him. The idea that God is relational and desires intimacy with us is one of the first things we learn about Him in Genesis. At the end of God's Book, we read about the re-creation of paradise as a place where He chooses again to dwell with His people. Revelation 22:3 even suggests God will relocate His throne to the new Jerusalem, another reason He makes all things new. Between now and then, He indwells all believers in the person of the Holy Spirit. Man, the dwelling place of God! That's enough to blow our minds wide open.

All of this points to God's love for us. He expends great effort to make all things new and re-create paradise because He loves us and wants to be with us. As an earthly father I understand this sentiment because one day my own kids will leave our home, go to college, get a job, get married, and start their own families—hopefully in that order. I want my kids to fulfill every purpose for which God created them, no matter where that takes them on this earth. But I love them so much that I dream about building a big enough house in a perfect place where we can all live together as one big family. Wouldn't that be great! I know what you're thinking. Dream on. I will, and then I remember that's exactly the place Jesus is preparing for us called heaven, the Father's big house where we can all live together with Him in a perfect paradise.

A Few Things Missing in Heaven

By the way, you'll be glad to know some things are missing in the new heaven, which is part of what makes it a perfect paradise. For example, Revelation 21:4 says, "Death shall be no more." Can somebody shout hallelujah? One day the lake of fire will swallow up death and Hades. The late author and renowned Bible teacher J. Oswald Sanders says, "The king of terrors, the last enemy, will never be able to breach the pearly gates and disturb the bliss of heaven! No more deathbed vigils or funerals. The hearse will have made its last journey."[34]

Verse 4 also tells us, "He will wipe away every tear from their eyes… neither shall there be mourning, nor crying, nor pain anymore, for the former things have passed away." That sounds so heavenly, doesn't it? As mentioned earlier in the book, I take this to mean God will selectively adjust our painful memories. Either the ecstatic joy of heaven will eclipse all sorrow or God will totally remove even the memory of friends and loved ones that rejected Jesus and ended up in a place of eternal torment.

There's more that's missing. Because I love the beach and the ocean so much, I'm sad to read "the sea was no more" (Revelation 21:1). But apparently there's no need for the oceans in the new heaven. Water covers nearly seventy-five percent of the present earth. But the new earth will need much more inhabitable space. Pain is missing from heaven too. No heartaches or headaches. Neither Tylenol nor Advil will be needed in the holy city. And we won't find a single wicked person in heaven nor a smidgen of corruption. Revelation 21:8 says,

> But as for the cowardly, the faithless, the detestable, as for murderers, the sexually immoral, sorcerers, idolaters, and all liars, their portion will be in the lake that burns with fire and sulfur, which is the second death.

It's hard for us to imagine a world with no sin, no spinning of lies, no murders, no pornography, no pagan worship and the like. The present world is viciously corrupt, but all of that is missing in heaven. Verse 27 drives home the point further: "Nothing unclean will ever enter it, nor anyone who does what is detestable or false, but only those who are written in the Lamb's book of life."

Is your name written in the Lamb's book of life? Possessing faith in the Lord Jesus Christ is the only way to make sure your name is not among the missing in heaven.

Finally, the Bible says there is no temple in heaven, nor is there a sun or a moon.

> And I saw no temple in the city, for its temple is the Lord God the Almighty and the Lamb. And the city has no need of sun or moon to shine on it, for the glory of God gives it light, and its lamp is the Lamb. By its light will the nations walk, and the kings of the earth will bring their glory into it, and its gates will never be shut by day—and there will be no night there. They will bring into it the glory and the honor of the nations (Revelation 21:22-26).

In the Old Testament, the glory of God resided in a place called the holy of holies inside a temporary worship structure called the tabernacle, and then later in the temple built by Solomon. In the New Testament, believers' bodies are the temple of the Holy Spirit (1 Corinthians 6:19-20). God made us His dwelling place! During the future Millennium following the Tribulation period on earth, the temple will be rebuilt. But in the eternal state, which is also the new heaven, there is no temple because the Lord God Himself and Jesus, the Lamb of God, are the temple. For all of eternity, the saints of God are in the perfect presence of God. There is no need for a special structure where we can go and worship God. In heaven, His glorious presence and our everyday life will be seamless.

So what's up with the missing sun and moon? Because God is light, there is no need for substitute luminaries like the sun and moon. And because God is light all of the time, there is no darkness in heaven; it is constantly daytime. That's one reason the Bible says believers are "people of the day." I also take this to mean we will not sleep in heaven. Like the angels, our perfected bodies will not need rest even though our lives will be full of continuous activity.

In what way will the kings of the earth bring their glory into the heavenly city? The preposition "into" not "to" is perhaps used to indicate that whatever glory the Gentile kings might have had on earth will be overshadowed by and submitted to the glory of God. Certainly, no person will live for his own glory in heaven. All glory and honor belong to the Glorious One.

Are you beginning to like new things as much as I do?

15

Imagine There's a Heaven

Some things in life are completely beyond description. For example, after returning from a particularly stunning vacation location like the Hawaiian Islands, words fail us as we try to explain to friends what we saw and experienced. Photos help. Some pictures are truly worth a thousand words. However, we quickly say things like, "You just had to be there!"

Recently, this happened to me while leading a "Something Good Radio" tour of the seven churches of Asia Minor. After visiting the ancient places of worship located along the western coast of modern day Turkey, we set sail for Athens. Along the way, we stopped off at some of the beautiful Greek islands located in the midnight blue Mediterranean Sea. Santorini Island was everyone's favorite. Alluring black sand beaches, breathtaking beauty, incredible outdoor restaurants, ancient cities, and an active volcano are some of the reasons people travel to this exotic place from all around the world. As our ship slowly approached the land mass, it was like experiencing a living postcard. In fact, most travel brochures that advertise trips to the Greek islands use a view from the high cliffs of Santorini to entice travelers. It's not hard to see why.

Our ship anchored in the bay and we disembarked into smaller boats that took us to shore. Once in port, we rode the cable car up the steep mountain to the top of the island where hotels, restaurants, and other beautiful whitewashed buildings with blue, domed rooftops virtually hang on the cliffs overlooking the sea below. From there, I called my wife. Sadly, Cathryn was not able to join me on this spiritual tour. She stayed home with our two school-age children. My first words to her were, "I'm standing in the place where we must come to enjoy our second honeymoon. I wish you were here right now."

As I tried to describe to my wife the spectacular scene before my eyes, words indeed failed me. The best I could do was bring home an artist's painting of a typical view of Santorini, if there is such a thing. I found it in one of the quaint shops during my brief visit to the island paradise. We framed the eight-by-ten canvas and today it hangs in our bedroom as a reminder of where we soon plan to celebrate the blessings of a long, fruitful marriage.

The Bible says, "No eye has seen, no ear has heard, and no mind has imagined what God has prepared for those who love him" (1 Corinthians 2:9 NLT). That means Santorini is not heaven; it's not even close to what I can only imagine in my mind about heaven. Heaven is better than any place we might believe is the most heavenly place on earth.

Beatles legend John Lennon told us to imagine there's no heaven. Instead, let's allow our imaginations of heaven to run like wild horses. Yes, imagine there's a heaven; it's easy if we open the pages of Scripture to the Revelation of Jesus Christ and read another of John's description of the holy city.

IMAGINE A MASSIVE PLACE

We've already established that heaven is the Father's big house. Jesus said it has "many rooms," leading Christians for centuries to sing about their "mansion in the sky" (John 14:1-3). Revelation 21–22 gives one of the most detailed descriptions of heaven found anywhere in the Bible. Let's return there for a description of its size.

> Then came one of the seven angels who had the seven bowls full of the seven last plagues and spoke to me, saying,

> "Come, I will show you the Bride, the wife of the Lamb." And he carried me away in the Spirit to a great, high mountain, and showed me the holy city Jerusalem coming down out of heaven from God, having the glory of God, its radiance like a most rare jewel, like a jasper, clear as crystal. It had a great, high wall, with twelve gates, and at the gates twelve angels, and on the gates the names of the twelve tribes of the sons of Israel were inscribed—on the east three gates, on the north three gates, on the south three gates, and on the west three gates. And the wall of the city had twelve foundations, and on them were the twelve names of the twelve apostles of the Lamb. And the one who spoke with me had a measuring rod of gold to measure the city and its gates and walls. The city lies foursquare, its length the same as its width. And he measured the city with his rod, 12,000 stadia. Its length and width and height are equal. He also measured its wall, 144 cubits by human measurement, which is also an angel's measurement (Revelation 21:9-17).

Words didn't fail John when the angel of the Lord showed him "the holy city Jerusalem coming down out of heaven from God" (v. 10). The Holy Spirit gave him every word the Father wants us to know about the heavenly city, even though John's description leaves us desiring to know more. One sense we get from the Apocalypse is that heaven is a massive place.

For example, John says the length, width, and height of the city are each 12,000 stadia. What is a stadia? A stadia is an ancient Greek and Roman measurement that equals about six hundred seven feet. So, imagine something like a cube approximately 1500 miles up, down, and across. As mentioned in an earlier chapter, that's the distance from the eastern seaboard of the United States to the Rocky Mountains, or from the southernmost tip of Florida to Maine.

John goes on to say the wall of the city is one hundred forty-four cubits. How long is a cubit? The length of a cubit was based on the distance from the elbow to the fingertips and varied between different ancient people groups (approximately seventeen to twenty inches).[35] So, if my math is correct, the city's wall is the height of a twenty-four-story building. Are you beginning to get a sense of the grandness of the heavenly city? In his book *The Wonder of Heaven,* author Ron Rhodes notes,

> Someone calculated that if this structure is cube-shaped, it would allow for 20 billion residents, each having his or her own private 75-acre cube. If each residence were smaller, then there is room to accommodate 100 thousand billion people, Even then, plenty of room is left over for parks, streets, and other things you would see in any normal city.[36]

IMAGINE A WELCOMING PLACE

John mentions twelve gates and twelve foundations. That makes three entries on each of the four sides of the cubed city. Architecturally, the city provides for easy entrance from any place on the new earth. The fact that gates are present implies there's inhabitable space inside and outside the city, and God's people will experience both spaces as they freely flow in and out of the new Jerusalem. And because heaven is a perfect place with nothing to defile it, the large and beautiful gates remain open perpetually (Revelation 21:25-27).

Stationed at each of the twelve gates is one angel, placed there presumably as an honor guard and a welcoming committee of one. Can you imagine an angel from heaven greeting you each time you walk through one of heaven's gates? That's what I call a hospitality team! Most churches work hard to put the friendliest people in the congregation at the doors of the church when people arrive and depart. The multiple entries into the holy city, plus the angelic greeters makes heaven a most welcoming place to live.

There's more that makes heaven a welcoming place. Above each of the gates leading into the new Jerusalem is the name of one of the twelve tribes of Israel. Some Bible scholars believe this is a reminder that "salvation is from the Jews," something Jesus declared to the Samaritan woman He met at Jacob's well (John 4:22). This idea dates back to the time when God told Abram, "And I will make of you a great nation, and I will bless you and make your name great, so that you will be a blessing...and in you all the families of the earth shall be blessed" (Genesis 12:2-3). The Messianic line is Jewish from Abraham all the way to Jesus of Nazareth. In other words, Christianity has deep Jewish roots! This is something Gentile believers must never forget in the present life and will never forget in the life to come.

Furthermore, the names of the twelve apostles are written on the twelve foundations of the city. Perhaps this too is a reminder of the role the apostles played in the start-up of the church as Paul mentions in his letter to the Ephesians (2:20). The inscriptions here and on the gates will remind inhabitants of heaven for all of eternity that our spiritual heritage is both Jew and Gentile. Both are welcome in God's forever family.

Obviously the number twelve plays a prominent role in the description of the new Jerusalem. Twelve angels are posted at twelve city gates, each made of a single pearl (twelve pearls in all) and marked by the names of the twelve tribes of Israel. Furthermore, there are twelve foundations inscribed by the names of the twelve apostles. And don't forget the tree of life reappears in Revelation 22, bearing twelve delicious fruits for each month of the year. Sounds like paradise, doesn't it?

All of this points to the fact that God is a grand master of details and calculated precision. It took the Lord God of heaven and earth six days to create the incredible world in which we live and the cosmos beyond. The Carpenter from Nazareth has been preparing the new paradise for at least two thousand years (John 14:1-3). We can only imagine its beauty and detail.

Imagine a Beautiful Place

The angel of the Lord compared the holy city to a beautiful bride by saying to John, "Come, I will show you the Bride, the wife of the Lamb" (Revelation 21:9). Now a city is not a bride and vice versa, but I think we can all agree there's nothing more beautiful and glorious than a bride on her wedding day. I think about that every time I look at my wife's wedding portrait. Is there a better analogy of beauty the angel could have used?

Of course, the bride the angel put on display is the church that in the New Testament is also called the bride of Christ. A city without inhabitants is an empty shell. But when the holy city is inhabited by the "holy ones" of God, apparently there is no sight more beautiful in all of God's creation. John added layers of beauty by describing the descending city as "having the glory of God, its radiance like a most rare jewel, like a jasper, clear as crystal." A bride dressed in rare and radiant jewels. Really, is anything more beautiful?

A few verses later, John expands the dazzling description by saying, "The wall was built of jasper, while the city was pure gold, like clear glass. The foundations of the wall of the city were adorned with every kind of jewel" (Revelation 21:18-19). What he writes next sounds like an enchanting trip to Tiffany & Co. of New York as he mentions jasper, sapphire, agate, emerald, onyx, carnelian, chrysolite, beryl, topaz, chrysoprase, jacinth, amethyst, and twelve gates, each made of a single pearl. "And," he adds, "the street of the city was pure gold, like transparent glass" (v. 21). No ugly concrete or asphalt in paradise, and no potholes! What we consider beautiful and precious stones will be common building materials in heaven.

The late fiery Baptist preacher W.A. Criswell unpacks the imagery even further by noting, "The entire city of splendor proclaims God's covenant relationship with the bride of the Lamb—His people Israel and His redeemed Church."[37] Yes, heaven is all about the beauty of covenant relationship as pictured in the marriage union between one man and one woman, which God created as a divine institution from the very beginning to demonstrate His eternal love (Genesis 1–2). The glory of God in heaven is one reason we must always protect the sanctity of marriage, and the same reason the devil relentlessly attacks it.

Heaven is also a place where we will experience true beauty with all its divine allure. Thinking people in every generation have contemplated the essence of beauty. What is beauty? Is beauty universal? Is beauty anything more than aesthetic appreciation? Philosophers pose many questions but offer few concrete answers. "That's beautiful" is a common phrase we use in our casual conversations. But can we say with certainty what's beautiful and what's not? Is beauty truly in the eye of the beholder? Can beauty be turned into an industry and sold in a way that satisfies our deepest desires? And what are we missing as fallen creatures, though created in the image of God, when we exchange true beauty for cheap, worldly substitutes? Deep questions, I know. But let's go deeper into beauty with the help of C.S. Lewis who expressed serious thoughts about the subject in his book *The Weight of Glory*.

> We do not want merely to see beauty, though, God knows, even that is bounty enough. We want something else which can hardly be put into words—to be united with the beauty we see, to pass into it, to receive it into ourselves, to bathe in it, to become part of it. That is why we have peopled air and earth and water with gods and goddesses and nymphs and elves—that, though we cannot, yet these projections can, enjoy in themselves that beauty, grace, and power of which Nature is the image... At present we are on the outside of the world, the wrong side of the door. We discern the freshness and purity of morning, but they do not make us fresh and pure. We cannot mingle with the splendours we see. But all the leaves of the New Testament are rustling with the rumour that it will not always be so. Someday, God willing, we shall get in.[38]

Indeed, one day we shall mingle with the splendors John saw in heaven when the rumors rustling in the New Testament leaves become reality for us. At present we see beauty imperfectly, through fuzzy spectacles, and from the underside of a magnificent tapestry. We wait in faith and hope for the beauty that promises to fulfill us completely one day. And when that day arrives, when we step through one of heaven's jeweled gates and walk on her translucent gold streets, we will take it all in, breathing deeply until we become one with splendor. Until then, as Lewis says, we are like little children who too easily settle for "making mud pies in a slum because we cannot imagine what is meant by the offer of a holiday at the sea."[39]

Imagine a Healing Place

John's vision of paradise continues as he begins the final chapter of the Apocalypse.

> Then the angel showed me the river of the water of life, bright as crystal, flowing from the throne of God and of the Lamb through the middle of the street of the city; also, on either side of the river, the tree of life with its twelve kinds of fruit, yielding its fruit each month. The leaves of the tree were for the healing of the nations (Revelation 22:1-2).

The tree of life reappears in the new holy city with special leaves that heal the nations. Paradise lost is now paradise regained. The prince of preachers, Charles Haddon Spurgeon, says, "That paradise which the first Adam lost for us the second Adam will regain for us, with added bliss, and superior joy; we shall dwell where a river rolls with a placid stream, and surrounds a land where there is gold."[40]

Cathryn and I used to live in Cinco Ranch, a master-planned community on the west side of Houston in Katy, Texas. The ranch is far from heaven, but part of what we loved about living there was the beautifully manicured boulevards lined with fast-growing crepe myrtles that bloom brilliant colors from spring to fall. Multiply that breathtaking image a million times over when you think about beautiful trees of life lining either side of a crystal clear river of life flowing from the throne of God.

The tree of life is unlike any other tree we know. It yields a different fruit each month of the year, like a fruit-of-the-month club only better. And its leaves have special qualities "for the healing of the nations." Interpreters are divided on the symbolic versus literal understanding of the trees and river. There's no reason not to embrace both. Although there is no sickness or death in heaven, the tree's fruit and leaves seem to contribute to the overall wellness of people living in the eternal city. The word translated "healing" comes from the Greek word *therapeian* from which the English word "therapeutic" also derives.

In what ways do the nations experience healing? Certainly the absence of war, ethnic cleansing, tyranny, injustice, pollution, corruption, collapsing financial markets, disease, and more give way to healing. In some sense, healing will be complete but ongoing, our wellness deepening throughout eternity. For once, the nations of earth will truly be united as people from every tribe, ethnicity, and language will stand before the Lamb's throne and worship Him in perfect unity (Revelation 7:9).

Imagine a Worshipping Place

It goes without saying but is worth noting that heaven is a worshipping place. Revelation 22:3 (ESV) simply says, "And his servants will worship him." Since we were created for worship, and because the Father is always seeking true worshippers who will "worship in spirit and truth" (John 4:24), heaven will be a place where authentic worship happens perfectly.

John pauses three times in the book of Revelation to give us a glimpse of worship in heaven (4:8-11; 5:8-14; 7:9-12). While apocalyptic disasters are happening on earth during the Tribulation period, exhilarating worship is taking place in heaven. John's descriptions are breathtaking. For example,

> Then I looked, and I heard around the throne and the living creatures and the elders the voice of many angels, numbering myriads of myriads and thousands of thousands, saying with a loud voice, "Worthy is the Lamb who was slain, to receive power and wealth and wisdom and might and honor and glory and blessing!" And I heard every creature in heaven and on earth and under the earth and in the sea, and all that is in them, saying, "To him who sits on the throne and to the Lamb be blessing and honor and glory and might forever and ever!" And the four living creatures said, "Amen!" and the elders fell down and worshiped (Revelation 5:11-14).

What a fabulous picture! All of God's creation joins their applause in rapturous worship. John includes, "Every creature in heaven and on earth and under the earth and in the sea, and all that is in them." Did he leave out the rocks that Jesus said would cry out if we did not worship Him (Luke 19:40)?

In many ways, this life is a dress rehearsal for the life to come. That includes the way we worship. Whenever we gather with God's people for corporate worship, and when we enter into times of personal and private worship, we are practicing for one of heaven's grand worship experiences. Keeping that thought in mind might just transform the church on earth with no more business-as-usual Sunday worship!

I also get the sense that in heaven our worship and our work will become more integrated. There's no false dichotomy between the sacred and the secular in heaven like there is on earth. I say that because Revelation 22:3 (NIV) can also be translated, "And his servants will serve him." In heaven, we will no longer worship our work or play at our worship, but the work we do will truly be an act of worship as we serve the true and living God in His eternal abode.

Maybe you thought heaven equals the absence of real work. Sorry to disappoint you. Work has always been part of God's created order. God Himself worked for six days and rested on the seventh, establishing a healthy rhythm of life for humans.

One of the first responsibilities God gave to Adam was to care for the Garden of Eden. Even in paradise Adam worked. His work was not a burden but a delight, and work itself was never a curse but a blessing. Only after man fell like Humpty Dumpty into sin was the ground cursed and work became harder in a fallen world (Genesis 3). Can anyone who runs in the rat race every day disagree? But the dignity, purpose, and meaning found in work remains.

All in all, your work and mine matters to God! The paradise regained by the new heaven will, in many ways, mirror the original paradise for which we were created, including the opportunity to experience meaningful work and the responsibility that goes along with it.

What kind of work will we do? That remains a mystery, but Jesus left clues in His parables by saying the one who is "faithful over a few things, I will make you ruler over many things" (Matthew 25:23 NKJV). God is ordered in everything He does, and we will join His order as rulers in the heavenly city in a measure that is in keeping with how we faithfully served Him on earth. Some scholars speculate that the "many things" may also include responsibilities for the vast, unexplored galaxies God created. John Morris of the Institute for Creation Research, for example, asks, "Has God created this immense universe as our 'Garden' for eternity?"[41] Again, we must leave the answer to this question in the realm of mystery and say we do not know.

What we do know is this: there are no white clouds on which to sit passively in heaven. Nor will harps be handed out for us to strum during a long and boring retirement. Heaven is a productive place where both worship and work are meaningful and fulfilling. The Father is always at work and He will employ us in His joyful service where all of our eternal life is a worship experience.

Dorothy in *The Wizard of Oz* clicked her red heels together and said, "There's no place like home." She was thinking only of Kansas, but in one sense she was right.

There's no place like our eternal home called heaven.

16

WILL THE DEAD RISE AGAIN?

Sam Parnia is a critical care physician and medical researcher at Stony Brook University School of Medicine in New York. He believes raising the dead may soon become a medical reality. In his book *Erasing Death,* he says, "We may soon be rescuing people from death's clutches hours, or even longer, after they have actually died."[42]

As you might guess, both the medical and religious communities view Dr. Parnia's claims with skepticism. Parnia prefers to use the word resuscitation instead of resurrection to describe what happens when death reverses. He admits that resuscitation science has a dismal record, but he is trying to change that with his latest research and training. When I read the article about his work, I thought to myself how sometimes it takes a while for science to catch up to what God already knows and for medicine to near what God has already done. Frankly, there's nothing new about resuscitating dead people to life again.

According to Dr. John Walvoord, former president of Dallas Theological Seminary, "The Bible actually records seven miraculous restorations: a boy raised by Elijah; a boy raised by Elisha; three raised by Jesus (Jarius's daughter, the son of a widow of Nain, and Lazarus); Dorcas raised by Peter; Eutychus raised by Paul."[43] Walvoord explains these were not resurrections in the strict biblical sense because the people did not receive a supernatural body and they actually died a second time. Their experience is better described as a resuscitation or restoration. However, the future resurrection of the dead is well established in the pages of Scripture.

Before I unfold what the Bible says about the future resurrection of the dead, I want to clearly differentiate between three concepts related to the afterlife. I have already mentioned two of them, resurrection and resuscitation; the third is reincarnation.

Reincarnation is a popular concept found in Eastern religions like Buddhism and Hinduism that view life and the afterlife cyclically. It's the idea that a dead person returns to life as another person or life form. The quality and form of one's next life depends on how he or she lived previously. Of course, nobody wants to come back as a lesser life form like a cockroach. Neither the God of the Bible nor science support reincarnation.

Resuscitation is the term medical science uses when basic life functions (heart, lung, brain) return after clinical death. Reports of near-death experiences probably fall into this category and have perplexed scientists, medical professionals, and even some clergy. However, resuscitation is not what the Bible calls resurrection.

Resurrection happens when a dead person is raised to life again and receives a supernatural body. While recognizable, he or she has a new, resurrected body. This is something only God can perform and is unique to Christianity, which views life and the afterlife in a linear, not cyclical, manner. In fact, everything in Christianity hinges on the bodily resurrection of Jesus Christ who is called the "firstfruits" of all future resurrections of the dead.

Some far-reaching people deny that Jesus was ever a real historical person who lived on this earth. Others accept that Jesus was a real person, but they deny that His death on a cross actually happened. I learned this while visiting the famous Hagia Sophia or Blue Mosque in Istanbul (formerly Constantinople), Turkey. As I entered the structure that was once a Byzantine cathedral built by Emperor Justinian I in A.D. 537, I acquiesced to removing my shoes and then picked up a brochure about the Islamic faith that read, "Muslims believe that Jesus did not die on the cross at all. Allah saved him, and someone else was crucified in his place." The brochure titled "Jesus and Mary in Creed of Islam" and published by Istanbul Muftulugu then referenced the Qur'an to prove its point (4:157-158). The brochure also says, "There is no need for salvation from sin, for there is no original burden." For me, the brochure settled the matter about the lack of theological harmony between Islam and Christianity. The two faiths simply do not agree on the essentials.

Nothing could be more ridiculous than to deny that Jesus of Nazareth was crucified on a Roman cross. The fact of His crucifixion is well attested by people like Josephus, a trusted and impartial Jewish historian who lived during the time of Jesus's life. Besides, Jesus didn't need Allah to save Him from the cross. He went to the cross willingly, in perfect obedience to the Father who sent Him there to pay the price for our redemption, something nobody else could accomplish but the one and only Son of God. Still others accept that a historical person named Jesus lived on earth and died on a Roman cross, but they deny His bodily resurrection.

For two thousand years, orthodox Christians have believed the life, death, and resurrection of Jesus Christ actually happened based on "many infallible proofs" (Acts 1:3 NKJV), and that His resurrection is the firstfruits of future resurrections of the dead. Let's explore what the Bible says about the future resurrection of the dead, starting in the Old Testament.

What the Old Testament Says About Resurrection

The doctrine of the resurrection of the dead is more fully developed in the New Testament. However, Old Testament believers did have an understanding that one day the grave would give up the dead. For example, Job anticipated his own resurrection when he said, "For I know that my Redeemer lives, and at the last he will stand upon the earth. And after my skin has been thus destroyed, yet in my flesh I shall see God" (Job 19:25-26). If Job is the oldest book in the Bible as many scholars believe, then even early humans embraced their final destination by clinging to the hope of resurrection from the dead. King David also declared his belief in resurrection when he said, "As for me, I shall behold your face in righteousness; when I awake, I shall be satisfied with your likeness" and "the upright shall behold his face" (Psalm 17:15; 11:7).

The prophets Isaiah and Daniel provide the strongest statements in the Old Testament about the future resurrection of the dead. Referring to the resurrection of the people of Judah, Isaiah writes, "Your dead shall live; their bodies shall rise. You who dwell in the dust, awake and sing for joy! For your dew is a dew of light, and the earth will give birth to the dead" (Isaiah 26:19). This prophecy specifically says the bodies of Old Testament saints will rise from the earth, as does Daniel's prophecy relating to the end times.

> "At that time shall arise Michael, the great prince who has charge of your people. And there shall be a time of trouble, such as never has been since there was a nation till that time. But at that time your people shall be delivered, everyone whose name shall be found written in the book. And many of those who sleep in the dust of the earth shall awake, some to everlasting life, and some to shame and everlasting contempt" (Daniel 12:1-2).

Jesus, the Gospels, and the Resurrection of the Dead

During His earthly ministry, Jesus spoke often about the resurrection of the dead and even predicted His own resurrection several times. In Matthew 22, He addresses the Sadducees who didn't believe in the resurrection by saying, "As for the resurrection of the dead, have you not read what was said to you by God: 'I am the God of Abraham, and the God of Isaac, and the God of Jacob'? He is not the God of the dead, but of the living" (31-32). The Bible goes on to say they were "astonished" at His teaching.

In a story He told about a great banquet, Jesus talked about the resurrection of the dead as though it was a foregone conclusion. "But when you give a feast, invite the poor, the crippled, the lame, the blind, and you will be blessed, because they cannot repay you. For you will be repaid at the resurrection of the just" (Luke 14:13-14).

People always marveled at Jesus's teaching. Some marveled and believed; others were curious but walked away skeptical of what they heard. Jesus couldn't have been clearer about the future resurrections of *all* the dead when He said these words, "Do not marvel at this, for an hour is coming when all who are in the tombs will hear his voice and come out, those who have done good to the resurrection of life, and those who have done evil to the resurrection of judgment" (John 5:28-29). Jesus said there are at least two future resurrections: a resurrection of life for believers and a resurrection of judgment for unbelievers.

Over the years, I've learned that funerals are the perfect time to talk about the future resurrection of the dead. Jesus thought so too. When His friends Martha and Mary sent word to Him that Lazarus had died, Jesus showed up days after the funeral. Family and friends were still grieving. Martha was upset with Jesus because He hadn't shown up earlier. She thought He could have prevented her brother's death if He wanted to. That's when Jesus consoled her with these incredibly mean words if they weren't true, "Your brother will rise again."

Martha was quick to say, "I know that he will rise again in the resurrection on the last day." Three cheers for Martha! Her theology was well formed in her mind, but Jesus stretched her understanding further and even personalized it when He said these epic words to her.

> "I am the resurrection and the life. Whoever believes in me, though he die, yet shall he live, and everyone who lives and believes in me shall never die. Do you believe this?" She said to him, "Yes, Lord; I believe that you are the Christ, the Son of God, who is coming into the world" (John 11:25-27).

Martha's declaration of faith in Jesus the Christ is one of the most powerful in Scripture! Can you say what Martha said? Is your belief in Jesus as the Christ and in your own future resurrection as strong as hers?

JESUS PREDICTED HIS OWN RESURRECTION

The wide world of sports is full of bold predictions made by braggadocio athletes. For example, Muhammad Ali, known for his confident swagger, said he would knock the heavyweight boxing crown off the head of Sonny Liston in 1964, and he did! In the lead-up to the first Super Bowl in 1969, quarterback Joe Namath audaciously predicted his New York Jets of the AFL would defeat the mighty Baltimore Colts of the NFL, even though experts said the Colts would win by 18 points. Broadway Joe's prediction came true when the Jets won the game 16-7 in one of the greatest upsets in sports history.

Bigger than the most brazen-faced sports prediction was Jesus's foretelling of His own resurrection, only there was no hint of a bragging spirit in Him. He humbly spoke the truth to anyone who had ears to hear, and even to those who were not willing to embrace His claims. Frankly, anybody who says Jesus didn't talk about His own resurrection before it happened hasn't read the Bible carefully. So, let's take a closer look by starting with a response Jesus made to a question posed by the Pharisees.

> Then some of the scribes and Pharisees answered him, saying, "Teacher, we wish to see a sign from you." But he answered them, "An evil and adulterous generation seeks for a sign, but no sign will be given to it except the sign of the prophet Jonah. For just as Jonah was three days and three nights in the belly of the great fish, so will the Son of Man be three days and three nights in the heart of the earth. The men of Nineveh will rise up at the judgment with this generation and condemn it, for they repented at the preaching of Jonah, and behold, something greater than Jonah is here" (Matthew 12:38-41).

Jesus links the plausibility of His own resurrection to a story found in the Old Testament about a prophet that got swallowed by a big fish and lived to tell about it. Some find this amazing, which is why skeptics attack the story of Jonah as vigorously as they do the resurrection of Jesus Christ. Jesus's logic suggests that if Jonah is a myth, so is the resurrection of the dead. Nobody in his right mind would hinge the entirety of his case to such a flimsy story, unless the story was true.

The late Henry Morris was a Ph.D. scientist and founder of the Institute for Creation Research. He taught that the creation account in the Bible is true and that the story of Jonah in the Bible is both believable and plausible. But Morris admits to much skepticism surrounding the story. In his book *The Remarkable Journey of Jonah,* he wrote,

> The account of Jonah and the whale stands out as one of the most difficult stories to believe in the Bible. It has been the subject of extensive ridicule, the source of Hollywood caricature, and the brunt of many jokes. Skeptics focus their deepest criticism at the very concept that a man could be swallowed by a whale and live to tell about it.[44]

Dr. Morris is right. For a lot of people, the story of Jonah is hard to believe. But so is the resurrection of Jesus Christ. Guess what? Both stories stand up to strong and closer scrutiny if you have an open mind and examine the evidence without bias. Therefore, Jesus knew what He was doing when He first predicted His own resurrection by linking it to Jonah's story. But it wasn't the only time He predicted His resurrection. After Peter confessed that Jesus was the Christ, the Bible says, "From that time Jesus began to show his disciples that he must go to Jerusalem and suffer many things from the elders and chief priests and scribes, and be killed, and on the third day be raised" (Matthew 16:21).

Later, Matthew again writes, "As they were gathering in Galilee, Jesus said to them, 'The Son of Man is about to be delivered into the hands of men, and they will kill him, and he will be raised on the third day.' And they were greatly distressed" (Matthew 17:22-23). I can certainly understand why the disciples were distressed by what Jesus told them. But that didn't stop Him from saying it again. Matthew records yet another time when Jesus told His disciples that He would be killed by the authorities in Jerusalem and then rise again from the dead.

> And as Jesus was going up to Jerusalem, he took the twelve disciples aside, and on the way he said to them, "See, we are going up to Jerusalem. And the Son of Man will be delivered over to the chief priests and scribes, and they will condemn him to death and deliver him over to the Gentiles to be mocked and flogged and crucified, and he will be raised on the third day" (Matthew 20:17-19).

Suppose I walked around telling people that I was going to jump off a fifty-story building and soar like a bird. You might conclude that I was either a liar or a lunatic, that is, until I actually did it using a special "wingsuit." Today, according to *60 Minutes,* extreme athletes travel to places like Norway's Romsdal valley during the summer solstice to jump off some of Europe's tallest, sheerest cliffs and fly at speeds of up to one hundred miles per hour. They are not gods, but they are doing what some people thought was impossible—humans taking flight without the aid of an airplane.[45]

Jesus was and is God, and He did what humans think is impossible; He rose from the dead after three days in the belly of the earth just as He predicted He would. And yes, as I mentioned earlier, He is the firstfruits of many more resurrections to come. The New Testament talks about seven distinct times the dead will rise leading up to the end of the age. We'll talk about those resurrections in the next chapter. But for now, what if the dead never rise again?

WHAT IF THE DEAD NEVER RISE AGAIN?

If the dead never rise again, there are many consequences to consider. The first is that Christ Himself is not risen and Easter is based on a fairytale. To the Corinthians, Paul writes, "Now if Christ is proclaimed as raised from the dead, how can some of you say there is no resurrection of the dead? But if there is no resurrection of the dead, then not even Christ has been raised" (1 Corinthians 15:12-13).

If the idea of a dead person coming to life again in a new and resurrected body is an impossibility, then the story of Christ's own resurrection is a hoax. I'm not talking about extending life through resuscitation minutes, even hours, after a patient's basic life functions cease (the work of Dr. Sam Parnia and others). I'm talking about a person who is stone cold dead and in the grave for days, weeks, or years being brought back to life by the power of God. If that did not happen in the past and will not happen in the future, then Christ's own resurrection is more than suspect. Of course, skeptics have been trying for centuries to make that case without avail.

A second consequence is that the gospel of our Lord Jesus Christ is useless, the apostles are frauds, and we are still in our sins. Paul goes on to say to the Corinthians,

> And if Christ has not been raised, then our preaching is in vain and your faith is in vain. We are even found to be misrepresenting God, because we testified about God that he raised Christ, whom he did not raise if it is true that the dead are not raised. For if the dead are not raised, not even Christ has been raised. And if Christ has not been raised, your faith is futile and you are still in your sins (1 Corinthians 15:14-17).

Paul could think of nothing worse than misrepresenting God. He protected the integrity of the gospel by guarding his own integrity. In Paul's critically thinking mind, the dead never rising again leads to a lapse in his own integrity, which would most certainly lead to the crumbling of the entire gospel, not to mention the deception of masses of people. Worse yet, it means there is no remedy for our sins and the last enemy has the last laugh. Then the secular philosophers are right and the word "futile" captures the essence of a life lived by faith.

A final consequence is the loss of hope in this life. Despair is not the absence of hope. Despair settles in our soul like a dark shadow when we learn that for which we deeply yearn is unattainable or not true. In the DC Comics movie *The Dark Knight Rises,* Bane uses hope as a means of torturing Bruce Wayne in a hellish Middle Eastern prison. Through an audio-muffling mask that anesthetizes his own pain, Bane says to Batman, whose body is broken after a fight with a fellow member of the League of Shadows in the sewers of Gotham City, "Hope. Every man who has ventured here over the centuries has looked up to the light and imagined climbing to freedom. So easy…So simple…And like shipwrecked men turning to seawater from uncontrollable thirst, many have died trying. I learned here that there can be no true despair without hope."[46]

As strange as it might sound, the apostle Paul agrees with Bane (or let's hope Bane got the idea from Paul). There's nothing more disheartening than unfulfilled hope. Hope that is really no hope at all lengthens our despair. Paul writes, "And if Christ has not been raised…Then those also who have fallen asleep in Christ have perished. If in Christ we have hope in this life only, we are of all people most to be pitied" (1 Corinthians 15:17-19). If it is true that the dead will not rise, then there is nothing more despairing than placing a friend or loved one in a freshly dug grave.

What does it all mean?

Thankfully, Paul does not leave us in despair. He goes on to say in the very next breath, "But in fact Christ has been raised from the dead, the firstfruits of those who have fallen asleep" (v. 20). Hope bursts alive in our soul like a springtime field of Texas bluebonnets because the dead will rise again!

Now let's talk about when and how.

17

The Seven Resurrections of the Dead

Arlington National Cemetery near Washington DC is a beautiful place that honors those who served our nation. For people visiting the nation's capital, Arlington is one of the must-see places. The cemetery spans six hundred twenty-four lush, green acres where more than 400,000 active duty servicemen, veterans, and their families are buried. Up to thirty funeral services happen there on any given day, more than 7000 per year. The cemetery's website describes Arlington as a "final resting place." I beg to differ. If I understand the Bible correctly, one day every one of those graves will open up and the dead will rise. In the pages that follow, I will show you why I believe that will happen.

As we discussed in the last chapter, the future resurrection of the dead is met with much skepticism. But you can't read the Bible with any seriousness, especially the New Testament, and ignore the fact that leaders in the early church believed Jesus rose from the dead. They also believed His resurrection was a prelude to all future resurrections.

For example, the apostle Paul embraced the future resurrection of the dead. Everywhere he traveled on his missionary journeys, Paul personally testified about the day he met the risen Christ on the road to Damascus. His testimony was often met with skepticism, especially by those who didn't believe the resurrection of the dead was even possible. For example, Acts 26 records the time when Paul gave a stirring defense of his ministry before King Agrippa. Speaking truth to power, he asked, "Why is it thought incredible by any of you that God raises the dead?" (Acts 26:8). That's a great question and could be asked of powerful and powerless people living in any generation.

Paul went on to speak in detail about the divine encounter that changed his life. Toward the end, he pressed the king by asking him, "Do you believe the prophets? I know that you believe." That's when King Agrippa gave his famous denial. "In a short time would you persuade me to be a Christian?" In other words, not today, Paul, not today.

The Greek philosophers of Paul's day thought the resurrection of the dead was laughable. That's why Paul had little immediate success in Athens when he preached Jesus and the resurrection in the open marketplace. The Bible says, "Now when they heard of the resurrection of the dead, some mocked. But others said, 'We will hear you again about this'" (Acts 17:32). Not much has changed in people's reactions to the gospel over the past two thousand years.

Paul planted a church in a city called Corinth not far from Athens. Corinth was heavily influenced by Greek philosophy, which is why Paul wrote extensively about the resurrection in his first letter to the Corinthians. The argument the apostle makes in chapter 15 is the sine qua non of the gospel. In it he addresses the following questions: Did Christ rise? Will the dead rise? When will the dead rise? How will the dead rise? And why does it matter if the dead rise again? Having addressed the first two questions in the last chapter, let's proceed with the others by taking a closer look at 1 Corinthians 15.

When Will the Dead Rise?

> But in fact Christ has been raised from the dead, the firstfruits of those who have fallen asleep. For as by a man came death, by a man has come also the resurrection of the dead. For as in Adam all die, so also in Christ shall all be made alive. But each in his own order: Christ the firstfruits, then

> at his coming those who belong to Christ. Then comes the end, when he delivers the kingdom to God the Father after destroying every rule and every authority and power. For he must reign until he has put all his enemies under his feet. The last enemy to be destroyed is death. For "God has put all things in subjection under his feet." But when it says, "all things are put in subjection," it is plain that he is excepted who put all things in subjection under him. When all things are subjected to him, then the Son himself will also be subjected to him who put all things in subjection under him, that God may be all in all (1 Corinthians 15:20-28).

That's a mouthful for anyone to read and digest! And if you're like me, it leaves your head spinning. Skipping across a series of intellectual mountain peaks, Paul takes his readers on a thrilling ride through end-of-the-age Bible prophecy. He talks about the kingdom of God and how every authority and power will be brought in subjection under Jesus's feet until God is all in all. J.B. Phillips paraphrases, "Thus, in the end, God shall be wholly and absolutely God." Of course none of this is possible if Jesus is not raised from the dead.

Paul's big idea is that Jesus is the first to rise from the dead of all who sleep the sleep of death. He flashes back to something in the Old Testament known as the Feast of Firstfruits when the first part of the harvest was given to God as an act of worship. In that way, God's people acknowledged that the entire harvest came from and belonged to Him. The fact that Jesus's resurrection is first also implies there are more to come. In fact, did you know there are seven resurrections mentioned in the New Testament? Many people incorrectly assume there is one general resurrection at the end of the age. However, a careful reading of the New Testament reveals there are seven. Two of the seven resurrections have already taken place. Here's a list of the seven resurrections of the dead mentioned in the New Testament.

- Jesus who is the "firstfruits of those who have fallen asleep"
- The token saints in Jerusalem raised (Matthew 27:51-53)

- The "dead in Christ" raised at the Rapture (1 Thessalonians 4:13-17)
- The two witnesses raised during the Tribulation (Revelation 11:1-13)
- The raising of the Tribulation martyrs (Revelation 20:4-6)
- The raising of the Old Testament saints (Daniel 12:1-2)
- The raising of the wicked dead at the final judgment (Revelation 20:11-15)

The first resurrection happened when Jesus, as He predicted, rose from the dead three days after He died on the cross. However, the Bible mentions another resurrection took place almost simultaneously. Read about it slowly and carefully in Matthew 27:51-53.

> And behold, the curtain of the temple was torn in two, from top to bottom. And the earth shook, and the rocks were split. The tombs also were opened. And many bodies of the saints who had fallen asleep were raised, and coming out of the tombs after his resurrection they went into the holy city and appeared to many.

Imagine the look of shock on the faces of the priests serving at the temple that day. The thick veil that separated the holy of holies from the rest of the temple split in two, "from top to bottom" the Bible says. It's as though God Himself reached down from heaven and tore it with His own hands. Why did He do this? Because after the cross and resurrection, believers have complete and total access to the holy presence of God. There's no need for an intermediary like a priest. New Testament writers go on to establish what theologians call the priesthood of the believer (1 Peter 2:5; Revelation 5:10).

Matthew goes on to record how an earthquake split large rocks in two, almost as easily as a knife through butter. And, "the tombs were opened." Yes, dead friends and loved ones, now alive, simply walked out of their cold, damp graves. How eerie! Because this is the only reference in the gospels to this resurrection, many Christians who know the

Bible well are surprised to learn about it. Matthew mentions it without any explanation, and he doesn't tell us how many were raised. The scene reminds me of an episode from *The Walking Dead*, only these people weren't zombies. Presumably, each one of them received his resurrection body as Jesus did and were later transported to heaven. However, we can only speculate about that. In keeping with the firstfruits idea, God made this resurrection happen seconds after Jesus rose as a token of the harvest that is yet to come.

A third resurrection takes place when the church is taken up and out of the earth during something called the Rapture. I admit there is much debate about the details of God's prophetic program. However, after my own detailed study of Scripture informed by the writings of careful scholars, I understand that the Rapture of the Church is the next big event on His calendar. Paul has this event in mind when he writes to the Corinthians about the resurrection.

> Behold! I tell you a mystery. We shall not all sleep, but we shall all be changed, in a moment, in the twinkling of an eye, at the last trumpet. For the trumpet will sound, and the dead will be raised imperishable, and we shall be changed. For this perishable body must put on the imperishable, and this mortal body must put on immortality (1 Corinthians 15:51-53).

In 1 Thessalonians 4:13-18, Paul provides even more details about the Rapture and the resurrection that will take place at that time, saying, "The dead in Christ will rise first."

> But we do not want you to be uninformed, brothers, about those who are asleep, that you may not grieve as others do who have no hope. For since we believe that Jesus died and rose again, even so, through Jesus, God will bring with him those who have fallen asleep. For this we declare to you by a word from the Lord, that we who are alive, who are left until the coming of the Lord, will not precede those who have fallen asleep. For the Lord himself will descend from heaven with a cry of command, with the voice of

> an archangel, and with the sound of the trumpet of God. And the dead in Christ will rise first. Then we who are alive, who are left, will be caught up together with them in the clouds to meet the Lord in the air, and so we will always be with the Lord. Therefore encourage one another with these words.

The "dead in Christ" refers to believers in Jesus whose bodies are presently in the grave but their departed spirits are in the presence of the Lord awaiting their future resurrection. When the Rapture happens, the dead in Christ will rise first. Then believers who are alive on earth at that time will suddenly be "caught up together with them in the clouds to meet the Lord in the air," all of it happening as fast as the eye blinks.

Now don't confuse the Rapture with the Second Coming of Jesus Christ. They are two different events in Bible prophecy separated by a seven-year period known as the Tribulation. One difference is believers meet the Lord in the air during the Rapture while the Bible says Jesus will plant His feet on the Mount of Olives at His Second Coming. Also, the Rapture will happen so quickly that only believers will see Jesus. However, the whole world will see Jesus when He arrives at His Second Coming to establish His millennial kingdom on earth.

The Bible mentions a fourth resurrection that takes place near the end of the Tribulation. During the Tribulation, also known as "Jacob's trouble," various people will give powerful witness to the gospel. Among them are two witnesses mentioned in Revelation 11:1-13. Based on the description found in this passage, some Bible scholars believe these witnesses are Moses and Elijah.

According to Scripture, the Antichrist will kill the two witnesses and leave their bodies in the streets of Jerusalem for three and a half days. Social media and other modern technologies make it possible for the whole world to see these murdered witnesses of the living God laying in the streets of the holy city. After three and a half days pass, something amazing will happen. The Bible says God will bring them back to life and transport them to heaven. The apostle John sees all of this happening in a vision and then writes, "They went up to heaven in a cloud, while their enemies looked on" (Revelation 11:12 NIV). John also saw a severe earthquake killing seven thousand people, leaving some survivors terrified and others praising God.

Chills run up and down my spine whenever I read what the Bible says will happen at the end of the age. This scene will immediately become "breaking news" on radio and television. Social media will jam up with photos and streaming video of the two witnesses standing up and walking around. Every television network in the world will interrupt regular programming to tell the story of two dead people in Jerusalem coming back to life. All of it makes me want to shout hallelujah and amen as I see the resurrected Jesus winning the victory for His people.

But there are three more resurrections to talk about, including yours, if you die before Jesus returns. Are you ready for the rest of the journey to the end of the age and your final destination?

18

Can God Resurrect a Cremated Body?

A careful reading of the New Testament reveals that God will raise the dead in groups—seven groups to be exact, starting with His one and only Son Jesus. From that first resurrection more than two thousand years ago, six others spawn to raise all the dead throughout all history and in every generation.

Some will rise from the dead to eternal life and others to everlasting death (the second death in hell), an idea admittedly difficult to embrace. In the last chapter, we discussed the first four resurrections, two of which have already happened. As we turn our attention to the remaining three, let's also ask how will the dead rise, why does it matter if the dead rise, and can God resurrect a cremated body?

Are you ready to dive deeper?

Let's look at Revelation 20:4-6 and the fifth resurrection.

> Then I saw thrones, and seated on them were those to whom the authority to judge was committed. Also I saw the souls of those who had been beheaded for the testimony of Jesus and for the word of God, and those who had not worshiped the beast or its image and had not received

> its mark on their foreheads or their hands. They came to life and reigned with Christ for a thousand years. The rest of the dead did not come to life until the thousand years were ended. This is the first resurrection. Blessed and holy is the one who shares in the first resurrection! Over such the second death has no power, but they will be priests of God and of Christ, and they will reign with him for a thousand years.

This passage describes the resurrection of believers who are martyred during the Tribulation. Their faith in Christ is rock solid, evidenced by a concrete refusal to worship an evil ruler known as "the beast" or to be identified with him by placing a mark on their forehead or hands. Much speculation has been made about the "mark of the beast." Some suggest the mark is a type of microchip technology that is implanted under the skin, without which a person cannot buy, sell, transact business, or travel during the Tribulation. A generation ago, this would have seemed implausible. However, such technology is already available and is being discussed for application in the world today. A one-world dictator like the Antichrist, empowered by Satan himself, could certainly use it to control masses of people and the world economy.

But if all believers are taken out of this earth at the Rapture, how is it that followers of Jesus are beheaded during the Tribulation? The simple answer is that people will come to faith in Christ during the Tribulation and many of them will be killed, actually "beheaded for the testimony of Jesus," John says. With the recent rise in beheadings conducted by Islamic terrorists in the Middle East, it's not hard to imagine such gruesome killings. However, these martyrs will enjoy a special resurrection prior to the Millennium when they will reign with Christ for one thousand years. Some confusion exists about why John says "this is the first resurrection." It appears he means "first" in the sense that it comes before the resurrection of the wicked dead, which occurs later at the end of the millennial reign of Jesus. It's not to be confused with Jesus being the firstfruits of all resurrections.

Daniel 12:1-2 indicates a sixth resurrection happening after Israel's "time of distress." This is when Old Testament saints like Abraham,

Isaac, Jacob, and Joseph come out of the grave. It's hard to pinpoint whether this resurrection happens before or after the resurrection of Tribulation martyrs. But the Old Testament saints rise from the dead in time to enter the Millennium and reign with Jesus on the earth for one thousand years. Yes, this includes King David, Moses, Samuel, and Daniel, plus anybody else in the Old Testament who, like them, were counted as righteous because they did not waver in their faith concerning the promises of God (Romans 4:20-22). Hebrews 11 mentions the names of other prominent Old Testament saints that will rise from the dead at this time. After the Millennium is when the seventh and final resurrection takes place. John writes about it in Revelation 20:11-15.

> Then I saw a great white throne and him who was seated on it. From his presence earth and sky fled away, and no place was found for them. And I saw the dead, great and small, standing before the throne, and books were opened. Then another book was opened, which is the book of life. And the dead were judged by what was written in the books, according to what they had done. And the sea gave up the dead who were in it, Death and Hades gave up the dead who were in them, and they were judged, each one of them, according to what they had done. Then Death and Hades were thrown into the lake of fire. This is the second death, the lake of fire. And if anyone's name was not found written in the book of life, he was thrown into the lake of fire.

This sobering scene is known as the Great White Throne Judgment where the unbelieving dead are finally raised and then judged. John says even "the sea gave up the dead who were in it." That means even Osama bin Laden, whose dead body was dumped into the deepest sea, will be raised and he, along with the great and small, will stand before the throne of God.

How Will the Dead Rise?

> But someone will ask, "How are the dead raised? With what kind of body do they come?" You foolish person!

> What you sow does not come to life unless it dies. And what you sow is not the body that is to be, but a bare kernel, perhaps of wheat or of some other grain. But God gives it a body as he has chosen, and to each kind of seed its own body. For not all flesh is the same, but there is one kind for humans, another for animals, another for birds, and another for fish. There are heavenly bodies and earthly bodies, but the glory of the heavenly is of one kind, and the glory of the earthly is of another. There is one glory of the sun, and another glory of the moon, and another glory of the stars; for star differs from star in glory (1 Corinthians 15:35-41).

Because the future resurrection of the dead is a miracle that only God can perform, and because our finite minds find it difficult to grasp, Paul uses an earthly analogy to explain how all of this will happen. In fact, let's give God credit for the analogy. Like so many things He created, something in the natural realm illustrates the supernatural. That's why Paul wants us to think like farmers that plant seed in the ground.

When death occurs, the body goes into the ground like a seed. The seed in the ground dies in order to give birth to new life. The farmer does not destroy the seed; he merely plants it in the ground where it dies and decomposes. Jesus made reference to this when talking about His own imminent death on the cross saying, "Truly, truly, I say to you, unless a grain of wheat falls into the earth and dies, it remains alone; but if it dies, it bears much fruit" (John 12:24). Jesus's life, death, and resurrection has certainly produced "much fruit" and a lot more is coming!

This raises questions about the proper way to treat the body after death. Should the body be buried or cremated? What does God think about cremation? Can He resurrect a cremated body? How should a Christian approach the decision, and does it even matter? Should cost be a consideration when we die?

According to Tyler Mathisen of NBC News, "cremation is the hottest trend in the funeral industry." He spent months conducting research for a documentary on the business of death and learned that "every year in America, 2.5 million people die. In 2011, the last year for which numbers are available, 42 percent were cremated, according to the funeral directors association. That's double the rate of just fifteen years ago. In some states, largely in the West, the cremation rate tops 70 percent."[47]

Why is cremation on the rise in America? Cost is certainly one factor. Cremating the body can run one-third the cost of a traditional funeral with a casket and a burial vault. This option is attractive to people who feel the money pinch in a declining economy. But some say the secularizing of America has also contributed to the increase in the number of cremations. More than a decade ago, *USA Today* noted the drop in "religious barriers to cremation." Christianity's strong influence in the U.S. once provided that barrier for several reasons.

Cremation has always been associated with pagan nations and religions. Some cite Amos 2:1 as proof of its heathen roots, "Thus says the LORD: 'For three transgressions of Moab, and for four, I will not revoke the punishment, because he burned to lime the bones of the king of Edom.'" Likewise, Hindus and Buddhists believe the body is evil and wish to be free of it. For them, cremation makes perfect sense as they anticipate reincarnation, not the resurrection of the body. Christians who live in countries where Eastern religions practice cremation are almost universally against it, having witnessed the gruesome public burning of dead bodies. They say the practice lacks the dignity and honor given to a loved one whose body is buried in the ground. More developed countries cremate the body out of sight, but some say the process is no less gruesome or dishonoring.

I prefer the practice of burying the dead body because it goes best with Paul's analogy of planting a seed in the ground in anticipation of a future harvest. In that way, burial can give witness to one's Christian belief in the future bodily resurrection of the dead. Please know I am not suggesting that burial or cremation determines one's eternal destiny—not in the least sense. Nor does a Christian that is cremated lose his or her salvation any more than a pagan gains eternal life by being buried in the ground. Thousands of people are buried every year without thinking twice about the Christian belief in resurrection. Likewise, a growing number of committed believers in Jesus Christ are cremated every year and not in deference to reincarnation. Besides, regardless of how the body is treated at death, the soul lives on in eternity.

I humbly give voice to my conviction in favor of burial for those who might be making a decision about the future. There's no need to revisit the past if a loved one has already been cremated. At the risk of repeating myself, the method we choose does not affect one's eternal destiny or what happens on resurrection day. I only suggest that burial is the best way for Christians to give a final witness to their faith in anticipation of the future bodily resurrection of the dead.

As to whether or not God can resurrect a cremated body, of course He can. Nothing is too difficult for Him. The same God who spoke the worlds into existence *ex nihilo*, meaning out of nothing, can retrieve crushed up matter that is scattered throughout the ecosystem and remake it into a resurrected body. Ashes to ashes, dust to dust. God is not worried about what will happened on resurrection day even if someone's remains were scattered into the Potomac River, or if his or her body was dumped into the deepest sea and gobbled up by marine life.

Another reason I prefer the practice of burying the dead is because God Himself buried Moses near Mount Nebo. Deuteronomy 34:5-6 says, "So Moses the servant of the LORD died there in the land of Moab, according to the word of the LORD, and he buried him in the valley in the land of Moab opposite Beth-peor; but no one knows the place of his burial to this day."

If He preferred, God could have chosen another way to dispose of Moses's body. But He chose burial. Furthermore, almost every major figure in the Old Testament was buried upon death. Pastor and author Randy Alcorn notes,

> God said to Abram, "You will go to your fathers in peace; you will be buried at a good old age" (Genesis 15:15). Abraham buried his wife when she died (Genesis 23:19). Isaac and Ishmael buried their father Abraham alongside his wife Sarah (Genesis 25:9,10). Scripture records the burial of Rachel, Leah, Isaac, Rebekah, Jacob, Miriam, Aaron, Joshua, Gideon, Samson, Samuel, David, Solomon, Elisha, and others. We're told of Joseph, "So Joseph died...and

> they embalmed him, and he was put in a coffin in Egypt" (Genesis 50:26). Obviously it would have been much easier for them to cremate Joseph's body and carry around his ashes for forty years, but this was not the chosen way.[48]

Some might argue that the practice of burial in the Old Testament is merely cultural. However, the fact that Jesus's body was buried in a tomb is woven into the fabric of Bible prophecy and into the gospel message itself. The apostle Paul, for example, summarized the gospel to the Corinthians by saying, "For I delivered unto you...that Christ died for our sins according to the Scriptures, *and that he was buried*, and that he was raised on the third day according to the Scriptures" (1 Corinthians 15:3-4 NASB).

Others argue that cremation merely speeds up the process of the body returning to the earth's dust from which it came (Genesis 3:19). That is true, but the body belongs to the Lord and is the temple of the Holy Spirit for the believer in Jesus Christ. Should we dishonor the temple in which God chose to dwell by intentionally destroying it? God might choose to end a person's life by a terrible fire that incinerates the body, but that's His choice not ours.

Now let's return to Paul's analogy about the seed in the ground and think deeper about his analogy. The new life, which takes time to produce, is not the seed itself but the crop that comes forth from the seed. And what usually springs forth is more bountiful and beautiful than the seed. When applied to the spiritual life, this analogy from nature gives us every reason to anticipate a supernatural, resurrection body unlike anything an extreme fitness workout can produce. With all its increased capacity, it will truly be heavenly!

> So is it with the resurrection of the dead. What is sown is perishable; what is raised is imperishable. It is sown in dishonor; it is raised in glory. It is sown in weakness; it is raised in power. It is sown a natural body; it is raised a spiritual body. If there is a natural body, there is also a spiritual body. Thus it is written, "The first man Adam became a living being"; the last Adam became a life-giving spirit. But

> it is not the spiritual that is first but the natural, and then the spiritual. The first man was from the earth, a man of dust; the second man is from heaven. As was the man of dust, so also are those who are of the dust, and as is the man of heaven, so also are those who are of heaven. Just as we have borne the image of the man of dust, we shall also bear the image of the man of heaven (1 Corinthians 15:42-49).

This is the second time Paul mentions Adam in this discussion. That brings us to the fourth and final question Paul answers in this great chapter on the resurrection.

WHY DOES IT MATTER IF THE DEAD RISE?

As sinful human beings, we are linked to Adam. We inherited Adam's sin nature and the wages of sin that go with it called death. As in Adam all die. But in Christ, the second Adam, all are made alive. As Paul reminds us, "The first Adam became a living being; the last Adam [Jesus] became a life-giving spirit." Are you following Paul's logic so far?

Jesus defeated sin and the devil at the cross where He paid the penalty for our sins. And through His glorious resurrection, He defeated the last enemy called death. If we die before He returns, and if we belong to Him by faith, we have every reason to look forward to our own future resurrection, all because Jesus lives. Remember, His resurrection is the firstfruits of many more to come.

Now why does all this resurrection stuff matter as you live your life today? Keep in mind that Paul was arguing nose to nose with the greatest philosophers of his day. These were people who did not believe in the resurrection of the dead, let alone Jesus's resurrection. As the philosophers wrestled with the big questions of life concerning origin, purpose, meaning, and destiny, the best they could conclude was to "eat, drink and be merry, for tomorrow we die." In their mind, there was no resurrection of the dead. So, their advice was to live your life to the fullest without any regard to eternity because the here and now is as good as it gets. Paul counters that philosophy by saying,

> Why are we in danger every hour? I protest, brothers, by my pride in you, which I have in Christ Jesus our Lord, I die every day! What do I gain if, humanly speaking, I fought with beasts at Ephesus? If the dead are not raised, "Let us eat and drink, for tomorrow we die" (1 Corinthians 15:30-32).

Paul's point is that the dead are raised and that is why he put his life on the line for the gospel. That is also why he died to his own selfish desires every day. There is much to gain in the next life and Paul didn't want to lose everything by frivolous living, and neither should we.

In the previous chapter, I mentioned Arlington National Cemetery. Another impressive cemetery runs north-south between the Mount of Olives and the eastern wall of the Temple Mount and the holy city Jerusalem in a place known as the Kidron Valley. Many important events in biblical history have taken place there. King Asa, for example, burned the pagan idols and asherah poles in the Kidron Valley. Jesus left the upper room with His disciples and crossed the Kidron Valley to pray in the Garden of Gethsemane before His arrest and crucifixion. The Kidron Valley also plays a major role in Bible prophecies about the end of the age.

Today, the Kidron Valley is a huge cemetery filled with ancient tombs. People have buried the dead there since the time of King Josiah. A few years ago while on a visit to Israel, our Jewish guide told me that many Jews plan their own burial in the valley outside the holy city because they believe the resurrection of the dead will begin in the Kidron Valley when Messiah comes. They expect to be among the first to rise from the dead.

On the future resurrection of the dead, the Jewish guide and I agreed. But, of course, Christians believe Messiah has already come in the person of Jesus Christ. When Jesus returns, Jews will welcome their Messiah; Christians will welcome Him back. That's because Jesus will plant His feet on the Mount of Olives, cross the Kidron Valley, and enter Jerusalem as the King of kings. Are you prepared for that glorious day? The best and only way to prepare is by faith in the Lord Jesus Christ who is the firstfruits of all future resurrections.

19

Was John Lennon Right About Hell?

Two Johns (well, one John and one Jon). One was a singer and songwriter that helped launch a music revolution in the 1960s as one of the Beatles. The other was a giant among preachers and theologians during the Colonial Era. The first John asked us to imagine there's no heaven or hell...only sky above us. The other delivered a sermon that warned, "O sinner! Consider the fearful danger you are in." One was a British rock star; the other placed his hope in the Rock of Ages.

John Lennon. Jonathan Edwards. Two men with two different views of the afterlife.

About fifty years before the American Revolution, God used the Reverend Jonathan Edwards to spark an awakening of religious fervor at his church in Northampton, Massachusetts. The passion spread and the First Great Awakening changed the spiritual landscape of the colonies. Some say it also planted seeds for the birth of a new nation. Edward's famous but much-maligned sermon titled "Sinners in the Hands of an Angry God" is considered a classic of early American literature. And yet, consider how strange these words sound today.

> O sinner! Consider the fearful danger you are in: it is a

> great furnace of wrath, a wide bottomless pit, full of the fire of wrath, that you are held over in the hand of that God, whose wrath is provoked and incensed as much against you, as against many of the damned in hell. You hang by a thread, with the flames of divine wrath flashing about it, and ready every moment to singe it, and burn it asunder.

When was the last time you heard "fire and brimstone" words like that in a sermon? Edwards painted a vivid picture of eternal damnation as described in the pages of Holy Scripture, but he was not known for his fiery delivery. Stylistically, he was nothing like the emotionally charged evangelists that followed him years later. Instead, he chose to read his sermon manuscript while letting his words and the words of Scripture speak for themselves.

Edwards' sermon about sin, the judgment to come, and eternal damnation brought a deep conviction upon the colonists under his shepherding care, and it lit a fire that spread throughout the other colonies. However, more than two hundred years later, that spiritual fervency has grown dim. Some people like Lennon threw buckets of water on the fires of hell. Peter Kreeft and Ron Tacelli write, "Of all the doctrines in Christianity, hell is probably the most difficult to defend, the most burdensome to believe and the first to be abandoned. The critic's case against it seems very strong, and the believer's duty to believe it seems unbearable."[49]

Recently, hell became unbearable for a pastor named Rob Bell. Bell served as the founding pastor of Mars Hill Bible Church in Grand Rapids, Michigan. A creative and compelling communicator, he skyrocketed to fame and his church grew quickly to over ten thousand people. Throughout his ministry, Bell has written books and produced short, catchy films that make people think about spirituality in ways they never have. However, Bell abandoned hell and then abruptly resigned his pulpit to pursue a "broader audience" including a career in Hollywood scriptwriting. He now goes soul-to-soul with Oprah as one of her spirituality experts. The last book Bell wrote, titled *Love Wins*, is a classic denial of the doctrine of hell repackaged in postmodernism. When the publisher released Bell's book, yet another John chimed in. Well-known pastor and author John Piper of Bethlehem Baptist Church in Minneapolis tweeted, "Farewell, Rob Bell!" Others joined in by labeling Bell a heretic for embracing a mixture of universalism and annihilationism.

The doctrine of hell was also unbearable for Charles Darwin. Did you know Darwin had roots in the church? He was baptized in the Church of England and buried in Westminster Abbey, despite abandoning the Christian faith and developing his evolutionary theory to explain the miracle of life apart from a creator God, positing something he called "the survival of the fittest." Darwin pointed to the doctrine of hell as one of the significant reasons he left the Christian faith. He couldn't imagine why anyone "ought to wish Christianity to be true" and called hell a "damnable doctrine."[50]

Atheist philosopher Bertrand Russell also had difficulty with hell. He wrote a book called *Why I Am Not a Christian* and called hell a "doctrine of cruelty." He also blamed Jesus as "partly responsible" for so much cruelty in the world because He taught about hell. The philosopher said flatly, "I do not myself feel that any person who is really profoundly humane can believe in everlasting punishment."[51] At least Russell got one thing right: Jesus *did* indeed teach about hell.

Admittedly, hell is a difficult doctrine to embrace. If it exists, some say it's time to remodel hell with air-conditioning. But we should be more interested in what Jesus said about the place than what a rogue pastor, a scientist, or a philosopher believes about it. Like you, I have many questions about this aspect of the afterlife. What does the Bible teach about eternal punishment? Is hell necessary? Who goes there? Does God send people to hell? If hell exists, what kind of place is it? Is hell forever? And can we really know whether our final destination is heaven or hell?

Before I dive deeper into this important subject as it relates to the afterlife, I want to acknowledge the words of perhaps the greatest Christian apologist in the twentieth century. Francis Schaeffer said, "The doctrine of hell must be taught with tears." Indeed, this is the spirit in which I write and speak about this classic Christian belief.

HELL AND THE CROSS OF CHRIST

Let's suppose for a moment that the pastor, the scientist, the philosopher, and the rock star are all correct about hell. What impact does that have on our belief in the afterlife? What should we conclude about true Christianity, "the faith that was once for all delivered to the saints" (Jude 3)? And how do we reconcile hell with the teachings of Jesus? We must address these good and fair questions.

First, if there is no hell, the cross of Christ loses meaning. The Roman crucifixion Jesus endured was severe, and from it we learn something about the awfulness of sin, how it offends a holy God, and the necessity of a place called hell. In a well-written essay called "The Doctrine of Hell," Douglas Groothuis, a professor of philosophy at Denver Seminary, argues this point eloquently,

> In the cross of Christ the sinfulness of sin, the holiness of God, and the reality of hell are all writ large with the blood of the Lamb. Only through Christ taking on our hell through His death could sinners be reconciled to a holy God. Once this is understood, hell takes on a clarity not otherwise perceived. Apart from the cross, there is no hope for forgiveness or reconciliation. Hell is the only alternative.[52]

Hell only makes sense in light of a proper and biblical understanding of the cross of Christ. But what about those who believe the cross is foolishness? They reared their ugly heads in the first century and have appeared in every generation since. The apostle Paul refers to them as "those who are perishing" (1 Corinthians 1:18). They embrace tolerance, inclusivism, and relativism as their highest virtues, making God-fearing people wonder, "Whatever happened to sin?" as the famous psychologist Karl Menninger once asked. The kind of preaching that rarely mentions the cross and the atoning blood of Jesus Christ also leads us down this same primrose path of foolishness.

The perishing soul often talks about the cross of Christ in sentimental tones. I'm referring to those who view Jesus's death as nothing more than the tragic end to a beautiful life. When asked why Jesus died on the cross, they go on to suggest that jealous and powerful people were threatened by His popularity and used their political influence to execute a good man. They acquiesce that Jesus was the greatest moral leader who ever lived and believe we should try our best to live out His teachings. They say the best way to do that is by focusing more on His extraordinary life than on His excruciating death. To them, humankind's greatest need is not redemption, but therapy, and sin is a psychosis that can be treated. How dare anyone suggest that our relationship with God is broken by sin and requires redemption. This nostalgic view of the cross always makes light of our transgressions; it also ignores how Jesus and the apostles understood the cross.

Not once do the pages of the New Testament suggest Jesus was surprised by the cross. On the contrary, He clearly anticipated the cross and stated His own purpose in going there. And according to the apostles who were eyewitnesses to His life, death, and resurrection, Jesus's death upon the cross was not an accident. Nor is it something to explain away as a symbol of a selfless life. For those reasons and more, we should never hide the grotesqueness of the cross, or its rough-hewn edges, or the way the nails split open Jesus's hands and feet, spilling His blood to the ground. The cross is ugly and wondrous at the same time. It is bloody and beautiful. It is all at once painful and the perfect plan of God to redeem us.

Thus, the bloody cross of Christ is central to the orthodox Christian faith, which, even according to the Apostle's Creed, includes a belief in eternal damnation for lost souls. The Old Testament law required that nearly everything be cleansed by blood, and the New Testament affirms that without the shedding of blood there is no atonement for sin (Hebrews 9:22). Jesus "descended into the lower regions" so that we wouldn't have to. In other words, "For our sake he made him to be sin who knew no sin, so that in him we might become the righteousness of God" (2 Corinthians 5:21).

Hell and the Free Will of Man

The biggest objection to eternal punishment goes like this, "How could a loving God send people to hell?" This objection is a straw man for two reasons. First, it isolates one aspect of God's character (love) while ignoring others of equal strength and importance (justice, holiness, and wrath).

In a blog titled "Doing Away with Hell?" Albert Mohler Jr. notes, "Theologian Geerhaus Vos warned against abstracting the love of God from His other attributes, noting that while God's love is revealed to be His fundamental attribute, it is defined by His other attributes, as well."[53] Put simply, God is more complex than any single attribute.

My love for my children is without question. However, I will discipline my kids when they do something wrong. If I do not discipline my children, then I do not love them according to Hebrews 12:6-8. However, it's easy for a son to wrongly conclude that he is not loved because Daddy put him in time out. I'm not suggesting that hell is little more than the Father's loving discipline of His children. On the contrary, hell is the eternal home for those who die having never become a child of God by faith in the Lord Jesus Christ (John 1:12). My point is that we simply cannot elevate one aspect of God's character to appease our discomfort with the idea of hell.

This objection also assumes incorrectly that God assigns people to hell against their own will. However, the Bible clearly states the intention of God's will by saying, "The Lord is not slow in keeping his promise, as some understand slowness. Instead, he is patient with you, not wanting anyone to perish, but everyone to come to repentance" (2 Peter 3:9 NIV). If God does not want anyone to perish, then why hell? Part of the answer to that question is free will.

God went to great lengths to rescue sinners by sending His one and only Son to die in our place. He invites everyone by faith to receive His free gift of eternal life through Jesus Christ (Romans 6:23). However, He does not force His will on us. "But as many as received Him, to them He gave the right to become children of God, even to those who believe in His name" (John 1:12 NASB). This verse implies that some do not receive Jesus or believe in His name.

But what about predestination, election, and the sovereignty of God? Doesn't God choose some and not others? I don't pretend to understand everything about the mysterious interplay between the sovereignty of God and the free will of man (nor is it my intention to solve a 2000-year-old debate). I just know that both are represented in the Scriptures. Somehow God is sovereign enough to allow for the free will of man without compromising His sovereignty.

Perhaps an illustration helps. Suppose you contract a disease that could hasten your death. A team of highly trained doctors properly diagnose your medical condition and prescribe the necessary treatment. They are 100 percent confident that you will live if you follow their protocol. They are equally confident that you will die soon if you ignore the prescribed treatment. Fully informed, you discuss the matter with your family and then decide not to follow the advice of the medical experts. Respecting your decision, the doctors have no choice but to send you home to suffer the inevitable consequences. Are the doctors to blame when you die? Of course not. Then why blame God when you choose to reject His kind offer of salvation and then suffer the eternal consequences in hell? C.S. Lewis wisely said, "There are only two kinds of people in the end: those who say to God, 'Thy will be done,' and those to whom God says, in the end, '*Thy* will be done.'"[54]

Hell and the Holy Justice of God

We've already established that the reality of hell does not negate the love of God; instead, it affirms His holy justice. If there is no hell, God is not ultimately holy and just. Most people who reject the idea of hell do so with some relatively good person in mind whom they cannot imagine experiencing eternal punishment. Charles Darwin, for example, rejected the Christian belief in eternal death for those who do not believe because "that would include my father, brother, and almost all of my friends."[55] However, if you ask Darwin or anyone else who objects to hell whether Adolph Hitler, Mao Tse-tung, Osama bin Laden or any other really evil person should go to hell, they would at least pause to consider the justice of it all.

Author Trevin Wax helps us understand how justice and the judgment of hellfire are intertwined concepts when he writes,

> Justice and judgment are two sides of the same coin. You cannot have perfect justice without judgment. God cannot make things right without declaring certain things are wrong. It's the judgment of God that leads to a perfectly just world. Try to take one without the other and you lose the Good News.[56]

Suppose I punched you in the face and broke your nose. Chances are you would scream for justice. You might even bring assault charges against me and file a lawsuit. The wrongness of my action depends on an agreed-upon standard of morality and a legal system that reflects that standard. Otherwise, your nose might hurt, but both your outrage and the lawsuit are unjustified. Now imagine punching God in the face. He alone is the absolute moral standard and determines when humans who are created in His image fall short of His glory (Romans 3:23). Does God have the right to enact justice when we wrong Him? Is hell an appropriate measure of justice for offending a holy God? That second question is more difficult to answer without a full appreciation of the nature of holiness. It's also difficult to answer because, as Mohler notes, one of the reasons this generation has a problem with hell is due to our notion of justice shifting from retribution to restoration.

> Retributive justice has been the hallmark of human law since premodern times. This concept assumes that punishment is a natural and necessary component of justice. Nevertheless, retributive justice has been under assault for many years in western cultures, and this has led to modifications in the doctrine of hell… Retribution is out, and rehabilitation is put in its place.[57]

The beauty of the gospel and the reason it is truly good news is because God found a way to express His perfect love and justice at the same time through the cross, which yields retribution for sin (Deuteronomy 32:35) but restorative grace for the sinner who repents and believes on the Lord Jesus Christ. Somewhere within the mysterious tension between the sovereignty of God and the free will of man, the choice is ours between atonement and hell.

Hell and Compassion for the Lost

Finally, many Bible-believing Christians are practical universalists. By that I mean they live as though hell does not exist and everybody will eventually end up in heaven. Ask them if they believe in hell as much as they do heaven, and they will answer in the affirmative. However, they can't remember the last time they shared their faith or prayed with tears because they thought a friend or loved one might die without knowing the only Person who can rescue them from what Jonathan Edwards called "a great furnace of wrath, a wide bottomless pit." If the reality of hell does not motivate the believer in Jesus to reach the lost with compassion, what will? Where are the tears? Where is the evangelistic fervor? Where are the men and women who, like the apostle Paul, say, "Knowing therefore the terror of the Lord, we persuade men" (2 Corinthians 5:11 KJV)?

It's not enough to welcome and woo a lost world with the love of God; we must also warn people of the judgment to come. To this point, Professor Groothuis says,

> We must beseech God to alert both our non-Christian friends and the church at large to the reality of hell. Without this doctrine firmly in place, Christians will lose their evangelistic edge. And without a proper fear of God's holiness, no one should be expected to come to Christ for His gift of forgiveness and eternal life.[58]

So, the consequences of a disappearing or air-conditioned hell are great. But John Lennon is not right about hell, no matter how catchy a tune he sang. Edwards was more on point in picturing the lost sinner as dangling above the flames of divine wrath.

Now, with moist eyes and a warm heart, let's go on to explore what Jesus said about hell.

20

What Jesus Said About Hell

In a previous chapter I mentioned Robert Jeffress, the senior pastor of the historic First Baptist Church of Dallas, Texas, and the author of several bestselling books. One of his recent books was originally titled *Hell? Yes!* Admittedly, that's a provocative title even for an outspoken Baptist preacher. However, it might have been too disturbing because four years after the original printing of the book, it was released again under a new title: *Outrageous Truth: 7 Absolutes You Can Still Believe*. The toned-down version still includes a chapter titled "God Sends Good People to Hell."

Does He? What did Jesus say about hell? Jeffress notes,

> Thirteen percent of the 1,850 verses in the New Testament that record the words of Jesus deal with the subject of eternal judgment and hell. In fact, Jesus had more to say about hell than He did about heaven. Given Jesus's extensive teaching about hell, it is contradictory to say, "I accept Jesus as a great moral teacher or even as the Son of God, but I refuse to accept His teaching about hell." [59]

Hell is a real place of unimaginable pain and suffering. I say that without any glee in my heart and while simply resting on the full authority of Jesus's own words found in the Bible. In Luke 16, for example, Jesus told a true story about a rich man who died and went to Hades, which I wrote about at length in chapter 7. Jesus said the man was in so much agony that he cried out, "Father Abraham, have mercy on me, and send Lazarus to dip the end of his finger in water and cool my tongue, for I am in anguish in this flame" (v. 24).

Jesus also referenced the fires of hell in Mark 9:47-48 by warning, "And if your eye causes you to sin, tear it out. It is better for you to enter the kingdom of God with one eye than with two eyes to be thrown into hell, 'where their worm does not die and the fire is not quenched.'"

So serious is the threat of hellfire that Jesus encourages us to radically address even the slightest sin in our lives, pulling the worm and fire reference from Isaiah 66:24 for emphasis and applying it to eternal punishment. And in a brief parable that sounds like a scene from *The Deadliest Catch* on Discovery Channel, Jesus again references the fires of hell.

> "Again, the kingdom of heaven is like a net that was thrown into the sea and gathered fish of every kind. When it was full, men drew it ashore and sat down and sorted the good into containers but threw away the bad. So it will be at the end of the age. The angels will come out and separate the evil from the righteous and throw them into the fiery furnace. In that place there will be weeping and gnashing of teeth" (Matthew 13:47-50).

While some might use the word "hell" crudely and casually, Jesus made no offhanded references to the place of eternal punishment. He described it in serious tones and as a place of "weeping and gnashing of teeth." On at least eleven occasions, Jesus used the word *Gehenna* when He spoke about hell. Real places, both *Gehenna* and *tartaros* (only found in 1 Peter 3:9) are equivalent to hell and the lake of fire but different from Hades, the temporary place of departed spirits that I discussed earlier in the book. Bible scholar Michael Burer writes,

> The Greek word gehenna has an interesting history. It originally began as a Hebrew place name which meant "Valley

> of Hinnom." This valley marked the boundary between the two tribes of Judah and Benjamin (see Joshua 15:8; 18:16). Some Israelites participated in child sacrifice by fire in this valley (see 2 Kings 16:3; 21:6; 2 Chronicles 28:3; 33:6; Jeremiah 7:31; 19:4-5; 32:35). In the intertestamental period this valley became symbolic for a place of fiery judgment upon the wicked, and the location was often used as a place to incinerate refuse. By the time of the New Testament the name was used almost entirely as a symbol for the ultimate place of fiery judgment that awaits the wicked.[60]

The Valley of Hinnom's bad history only got worse when the chief priests bought a potter's field with the infamous thirty pieces of silver they gave to Judas Iscariot. That's why today the lush, green valley is also called the "Field of Blood" (Matthew 27:6-8; Acts 1:18-19). By referring to hell as *Gehenna*, Jesus was not saying, as some suggest, that hell is the worst we make of things on earth. Instead, He thought of hell as a real place of grotesque and unimaginable suffering.

Hell is also a place of eternal fire, but not the kind of fire that incinerates because even the worm does not die there. Of course, some still have a difficult time reconciling the love of God with the eternal fires of hell. Thus, if they don't deny the existence of hell altogether, they try to reduce time spent there by positing that the fires of hell, if they are real at all, eventually annihilate (burn out of existence) the inhabitants. That might make us feel better about hell, but it's hard to make that case from Scripture.

In addition to the "worm" references, the honest Bible scholar must grapple with the Apocalypse of Jesus Christ that says the beast, the false prophet, and the devil himself will be tossed into the lake of fire. This happens when Jesus returns to earth to set up His earthly kingdom for one thousand years.

At the end of the time in Bible prophecy known as the Millennium, the unholy trinity are released from the lake of fire to torment earth's inhabitants one last time (Revelation 19:20). The point is this: one would think that one thousand years in the lake of fire is more than enough to burn anyone out of existence. But as TV character Gomer Pyle famously said, "Surprise! Surprise! Surprise!" The beast, the false prophet, and the devil emerge very much alive! At the final judgment, they are thrown back into the lake of fire along with death, hades, and all of the unbelieving dead to suffer eternal punishment. This is called the second death (Revelation 20:11-15).

Like heaven, hell is eternal. Jesus had no problem mentioning both eternal life and eternal punishment in the same sentence when He said, "And these will go away into eternal punishment, but the righteous into eternal life" (Matthew 25:46). Jeffress notes this and then says, "If you shorten the duration of 'eternal punishment' by any amount of time, you must also equally diminish the duration of 'eternal life.' One minute less in hell for unbelievers means one minute less in heaven for believers."[61] I take no delight (nor does Jeffress) in saying hell is a forever place.

Dark and Gloomy

Matthew records three times when Jesus referred to hell as a place of "outer darkness." Once when He was amazed by the faith of a centurion, Jesus said, "I tell you, many will come from east and west and recline at table with Abraham, Isaac, and Jacob in the kingdom of heaven, while the sons of the kingdom will be thrown into the outer darkness" (Matthew 8:11-12).

Jesus also told a parable in which He compared the kingdom of heaven "to a king who gave a wedding feast for his son." One of the attending guests didn't belong at the feast and the king inquired as to how he got there. When the uninvited intruder was speechless, the king said, "Bind him hand and foot and cast him into the outer darkness" (Matthew 22:13).

Finally, Jesus taught in another parable that the kingdom of heaven was "like a man going on a journey, who called his servants and entrusted to them his property. To one he gave five talents, to another two, to another one, to each according to his ability. Then he went away" (Matthew 25:14-15). The first two men doubled the talents they received through investment and hard work, but the third man buried his talent (a measure of money) in the ground. When the owner returned and learned what each man did with his stewardship, he became indignant at the third man who wasted his opportunity. He immediately took the one talent away from him and gave it to the man who now had ten, and then said, "Cast the worthless servant into the outer darkness" (v. 30).

In each case, outer darkness is a terrible punishment. It reminds me of the time when the God of the Hebrews judged the Egyptians with ten plagues, including bloody water, frogs, gnats, flies, dead livestock, boils, hail, locusts, darkness, and finally the death of "every firstborn in the land of Egypt." Exodus 10:22-23 describes the arrival of darkness, the ninth plague, by saying, "So Moses stretched out his hand toward heaven, and there was pitch darkness in all the land of Egypt three days. They did not see one another, nor did anyone rise from his place for three days, but all the people of Israel had light where they lived."

Have you ever experienced total darkness? I have once in my life for about thirty seconds not three days. It was quite unsettling. Cathryn and I were traveling with the kids in Texas and we stopped to visit the Natural Bridge Caverns near San Antonio. A tour guide took us into an underground world of natural beauty to view stalagmites, stalactites, flowstones, chandeliers, and soda straws. It was truly amazing. When we reached the lowest point in the tour—180 feet below ground—the guide gathered our group into a single cavern and then turned out the lights. She took some time to prepare us for what we were about to experience because she knew it would disturb some of us, and it did. Not long after the lights went out, I could sense the people next to me fidgeting. Soon I could feel my own heart racing. When the lights came on less than a minute later, everyone breathed a sigh of relief, and some said, "That was really weird!" Darkness is punishingly eerie.

Hell is a dark and gloomy place. Jude 6 says, "And the angels who did not stay within their own position of authority, but left their proper dwelling, he has kept in eternal chains under gloomy darkness until the judgment of the great day." We were not created for such gloomy darkness and neither were the angels who followed Lucifer in the rebellion against God. At the present moment those fallen angels are chained up in total darkness though somehow able to tempt us to carry out the deeds of darkness.

Darkness makes most of us feel uncomfortable because we were created in the image of God and, thus, made for the light, which is where God dwells (1 John 1:5). But presently we live in a dark world, blackened by sinful rebellion lurking in the human heart. Some people get comfortable in darkness and actually learn to love it. A few sentences after telling us "for God so loved the world" in John 3:16, Jesus juxtaposed light and darkness as a metaphor for good and evil by saying,

> "And this is the judgment: the light has come into the world, and people loved the darkness rather than the light because their works were evil. For everyone who does wicked things hates the light and does not come to the light, lest his works should be exposed. But whoever does what is true comes to the light, so that it may be clearly seen that his works have been carried out in God" (John 3:19-21).

WHERE GOD IS NOT

Darkness in hell could also be a metaphor for the complete absence of anything good including the presence of God; hell is a place where God is *not.* Second Thessalonians 1:9 says, "They will suffer the punishment of eternal destruction, away from the presence of the Lord and from the glory of his might." This verse refers to those who do not obey the gospel of our Lord Jesus Christ. The apostle Paul paints a sobering picture of the triumphant Christ "revealed from heaven with his mighty angels in flaming fire, inflicting vengeance on those who do not know God" (vv. 7-8). At some time in the future, God who is full of goodness and grace removes Himself and His glorious presence from unbelievers for all eternity. That is hell enough.

In his letter to the Romans, Paul writes about a point where God stops pursuing humankind with His love. At best we can call His approach tough love. The phrase "God gave them up" appears three times in chapter 1, making it one of the most stunning passages in the Bible. Romans 1 is not a description of hell, but it is a reminder that sinful humans can cross a line with God by presuming upon His love and grace. What's even more frightening is that God will one day give up all unbelievers to the eternal fires of hell because they ultimately "exchanged the truth about God for a lie and worshiped and served the creature rather than the Creator" (Romans 1:25).

On earth, unbelievers get to enjoy the common grace of God even if they do not acknowledge His presence in their lives. Jesus taught us to love our enemies for the simple reason that our Father in heaven "makes his sun rise on the evil and on the good, and sends rain on the just and on the unjust" (Matthew 5:45). However, cool and refreshing rain will never fall on the inhabitants of the fiery furnace because God is not there to shower them with His grace. Again, the Bible says unbelievers will suffer eternal punishment "away from the presence of the Lord" (2 Thessalonians 1:9). This reality should make believers weep and then do everything we can to urge our family, friends, and neighbors to place their faith in Jesus while there's still time to respond to God's grace.

Sorrow and Angry Regret

In every one of the places where Jesus mentions "outer darkness," He also says, "In that place there will be weeping and gnashing of teeth." I take this as more evidence of consciousness in the afterlife; however, it's the kind of awareness one would rather not possess.

Bruxism is the term medical experts use to describe the act of grinding, gnashing, or clenching your teeth. Severe bruxism is brought on by emotional trauma, anxiety, stress, anger, frustration, or tension and can cause various disorders. Knowing that I will escape judgment before the Great White Throne of God by faith in the Lord Jesus Christ is comforting enough. But whenever I read the following words found in Revelation 20:11-15, it's not hard for me to imagine how unbelievers will experience a strong dose of emotional turmoil when they catch a glimpse of the eternal flames of damnation.

> Then I saw a great white throne and him who was seated on it. From his presence earth and sky fled away, and no

> place was found for them. And I saw the dead, great and small, standing before the throne, and books were opened. Then another book was opened, which is the book of life. And the dead were judged by what was written in the books, according to what they had done. And the sea gave up the dead who were in it, Death and Hades gave up the dead who were in them, and they were judged, each one of them, according to what they had done. Then Death and Hades were thrown into the lake of fire. This is the second death, the lake of fire. And if anyone's name was not found written in the book of life, he was thrown into the lake of fire.

I can hardly imagine the full weight of realization that will seize the unbeliever when he understands what he has lost and where he is going. The fact that there is no second chance will pile on the pain, bitterness, and regret. So will the memory of every lost opportunity to respond to the gospel in faith as it plays over and over in his mind.

What about those who have never heard the name of Jesus, let alone what He did for them on the cross? Romans 1 tells us "they are without excuse" because all humans have received natural revelation in creation. "For what can be known about God is plain to them, because God has shown it to them" (v. 19).

Some people also imagine that two minutes in hell is enough to soften the unbeliever's heart. Actually, just the opposite is true. Like quick-drying cement, anger and regret will settle into the jawbone of everyone who rejects the loving offer of salvation through faith in the Lord Jesus Christ. The gnashing of teeth will last forever.

If I could scare you out of hell, I would. Instead, I prayerfully plead with you not to remain indifferent to the clear warnings of Scripture about eternal punishment. The Bible adds to the urgency of the moment by saying, "Today, if you hear his voice, do not harden your hearts" (Psalm 95:7-8). Do you really want to gamble on the possibility that what Jesus said about hell isn't true? A philosopher named

Blaise Pascal once posited that all humans wager with their lives that either God exists or He does not. With an infinite gain or loss at stake based on a belief in heaven or hell, he concluded it was best to live as though God exists and that what He says about eternity is true. What's known as "Pascal's wager" is not a bad way to end this chapter. Heads we win; tails we lose.

21

The Believer's Day of Reward

The largest soft drink company on planet earth wants to reward you for drinking their popular brown sugar water and other related beverages. You can find My Coke Rewards codes under the caps of your favorite Coke brands, also inside the tear-offs of 12-packs and on multipack wraps, says the company. Buy a product and get a code. It's that simple. Codes mean points, and accumulated points mean rewards—a catalog full of rewards including gift cards to major retailers, movie tickets, magazine subscriptions, and a whole lot more. Sounds enticing, doesn't it? Why does The Coca-Cola Company do this? Because they think it makes you want to go out and buy more Coke.

The same principle applies in the Christian life. Most of us are motivated to act if we're promised a reward. Eternal rewards, in particular, should motivate us to live every day of our life by faith and in a way that pleases God and serves His purposes. Our love for God and experience with His grace should too. But don't ever discount the power of rewards. Read the Bible carefully from Genesis to Revelation and you'll discover how the Creator of heaven and earth rewards great faith, which is "the assurance of things hoped for, the conviction of things not seen" (Hebrews 11:1).

For example, God said to Abram, "Fear not...I am your shield; your *reward* shall be very great" (Genesis 15:1). The writer of Hebrews tells us that Moses "regarded disgrace for the sake of Christ as of greater value than the treasures of Egypt, because he was looking ahead to his *reward*" (11:24-26 NIV). Earlier in the same chapter, which is known as the Great Hall of Faith, the Bible says, "And without faith it is impossible to please him, for whoever would draw near to God must believe that he exists and that he *rewards* those who seek him" (11:6). The last book of the Bible ends with Jesus saying, "Look, I am coming soon! My *reward* is with me, and I will give to each person according to what they have done" (Revelation 22:12 NIV). Yes, it is part of God's nature to reward. Have you joined His eternal rewards program?

Our long discussion about the afterlife brings us to the wonderful but sobering subject of eternal rewards. In the Bible, something called the judgment seat of Christ is the place where believers come to have their works in Christ evaluated by the judge of all the earth. This judgment is not about our sins, nor a determination of whether we belong in heaven. Rather, it determines the quality of one's experience in heaven throughout all of eternity as well as what duties and responsibilities God will give to us as we serve Him.

If you are a child of God by faith in the Lord Jesus Christ, rest assured about your right standing before your Creator. Romans 8:1 says, "There is therefore now no condemnation for those who are in Christ Jesus." This means we are guaranteed eternal life by faith based on the gracious promises and provisions God made to us through the atoning blood of Jesus Christ. As believers in Jesus, we are justified and forgiven; we stand before God clothed in the righteousness of Christ.

However, the Bible also says, "For we will all stand before the judgment seat of God" (Romans 14:10) and "for we must all appear before the judgment seat of Christ, so that each one may receive what is due for what he has done in the body, whether good or evil" (2 Corinthians 5:10). There's no escaping this scrutinizing judgment! Believers can't call in sick or just not show up.

Indeed, we must all appear and be held accountable for what we did with the time, talent, treasure, and truth God gave to us during our one life on this earth. Make no mistake about it. Salvation is not *by* works but we were saved *for* good works (Ephesians 2:8-10). Thus, heaven will distribute or withhold eternal rewards based on at least three things: the quality of our works (Psalm 62:12; Matthew 16:27; Ephesians 6:8), the measure of our words (Matthew 12:36), and the motives of our heart (Jeremiah 17:10; 1 Corinthians 4:5; Revelation 2:23). This reality should make every one of us pause and reflect on our own life in Christ because an eternal reward is far more serious than any reward we might receive for drinking brown sugar water.

How Are You Building Your Life?

In his first letter to the Corinthians, the apostle Paul gives greater insight into what will happen at the judgment seat of Christ by comparing our lives to a building, a race, and a trustee relationship. Thus, there are three implications we can derive from this future judgment for believers. First, build your life in a way that glorifies God.

> According to the grace of God given to me, like a skilled master builder I laid a foundation, and someone else is building upon it. Let each one take care how he builds upon it. For no one can lay a foundation other than that which is laid, which is Jesus Christ. Now if anyone builds on the foundation with gold, silver, precious stones, wood, hay, straw—each one's work will become manifest, for the Day will disclose it, because it will be revealed by fire, and the fire will test what sort of work each one has done. If the work that anyone has built on the foundation survives, he will receive a reward. If anyone's work is burned up, he will suffer loss, though he himself will be saved, but only as through fire (1 Corinthians 3:10-15).

A children's story about the three little pigs comes to mind. Three little pigs each went out into the world to "seek their fortune." The first little pig built a house made of straw. One day a big, bad wolf came knocking on his door and demanded entry. The little pig refused to open the door. That's when the wolf huffed and puffed and blew the little pig's house down. The second pig built his house out of sticks and the same fate befell him and his house. The third and smartest little pig built his house out of bricks. When the big, bad wolf huffed and puffed, the house made of bricks stood strong. The moral of the story? Build your house out of bricks, not straw or sticks.

Of course, there's no big, bad wolf and the judgment seat of Christ is not a children's story, but the principle is the same. The idea behind Paul's analogy is to build your life on quality works, words, and thoughts that, when tested by fire, will have lasting value like gold, silver, and precious stones. Obviously, anything built with hay or straw is weak and easily burns to the ground. Wood structures can rot and go up in flames too. The opposite is true of the other materials which are also symbolic of the way we build our lives. Specifically, what are we to make of these symbols? Author Ron Rhodes says, "Perhaps the figure is intended to communicate that those works performed with a view to glorifying God are the works that will stand. Those works performed with a view to glorifying self, performed in the flesh, are those that will be burned up."[62] Furthermore, William Barclay writes, "We stand before God in the awful loneliness of our own souls; to him we can take nothing but the character which in life we have been building up."[63]

Does the fire imagery mean some will lose their salvation at the judgment seat of Christ? On the contrary, Paul is careful to say in 1 Corinthians 3:15, "If anyone's work is burned up, he will suffer loss, though he himself will be saved, but only as through fire." This verse requires theological precision as it speaks of the loss of eternal rewards, not the loss of everlasting salvation. As sobering as it might sound, some believers will enter heaven joyfully, but they will smell the singe of their own burnt-up works. Theologian Norman Geisler says, "Everyone in heaven will be *fully* blessed, but not everyone will be *equally* blessed."[64] "That's not fair!" you say. Fair or not, heaven will be heaven for everyone who is there by faith in the Lord Jesus Christ, but it will be *more heavenly* for some based on the rewards handed out at the judgment seat of Christ. And because heaven is a perfect place, we will not grow jealous of each other's reward. Instead, we will fully rejoice in how each reward glorifies Jesus no matter who receives it.

How Are You Running the Race?

Second, because all believers will appear before the judgment seat of Christ, we should run the race to win the prize. This is what the apostle Paul implores us to do in his first letter to the Corinthians.

> Do you not know that in a race all the runners run, but only one receives the prize? So run that you may obtain it. Every athlete exercises self-control in all things. They do it to receive a perishable wreath, but we an imperishable. So I do not run aimlessly; I do not box as one beating the air. But I discipline my body and keep it under control, lest after preaching to others I myself should be disqualified (1 Corinthians 9:24-27).

Paul had the Isthmian Games in mind when he described the Christian life as a race. The ancient city of Corinth hosted the games, which were a precursor to the modern Olympics. The winners of each race customarily received a crown of leaves to wear on their head. Of course the leafy crown decayed in a few days and became a worthless pile of compost. But Christians run in a much more important race called life and winners receive an "imperishable" crown.

Each event in the games had rules by which the athlete participated. As in today's Olympic contests, every athlete's greatest fear was to hear the words, "You're disqualified!"

These days, hardly a winter or summer Olympics happens without the IOC disqualifying an athlete that broke the rules. Names like Marion Jones of the United States, Ben Johnson of Canada, and Ara Abrahamian of Sweden are among the top Olympic athletes who lost their medals due to various rules violations. The apostle Paul envisioned the sad possibility of preaching to others and then hearing the words, "You're disqualified!" on the believer's day of reward. By disqualified, was Paul thinking about the threat of losing his salvation? No, rather a disqualified believer loses his "winner's crown." He gets to reside in heaven because of what Jesus did for him on the cross, but his eternal reward is taken away.

For this reason, Paul always ran the race called life with the finish line in view, careful not to do anything that might disqualify him from receiving his eternal reward. He ran with a healthy sense of fear, respecting the rules of the race and the One who made them. Like an athlete, he disciplined his body and made it his slave, and so must we (1 Timothy 4:7). He knew that one day he would stand before "the righteous judge" and give an account of his ministry.

Near the end of his life and race, Paul wrote these words to Timothy, his young protégé in the ministry,

> For I am already being poured out as a drink offering, and the time of my departure has come. I have fought the good fight, I have finished the race, I have kept the faith. Henceforth there is laid up for me the crown of righteousness, which the Lord, the righteous judge, will award to me on that Day, and not only to me but also to all who have loved his appearing (2 Timothy 4:6-8).

> Fight the good fight of the faith...I charge you to keep this command without spot or blame until the appearing of our Lord Jesus Christ (1 Timothy 6:12-14 NIV).

> Fight the good fight, keeping faith and a good conscience, which some have rejected and suffered shipwreck in regard to their faith. Among these are Hymenaeus and Alexander, whom I have handed over to Satan, so that they will be taught not to blaspheme (1 Timothy 1:18-20 NASB).

Paul ran the race well and finished with distinction. He had every reason to believe he would hear the words, "Well done, good and faithful servant...Enter into the joy of your master" (Matthew 25:23). For that reason, he provides a good example for us to follow.

Tragically, two people named Hymenaeus and Alexander top the list of those in Scripture that did not run the race well or fight the good fight. Of course, the best example for us to follow is Jesus. The writer of Hebrews urges us to "run with endurance the race that is set before us, looking to Jesus, the founder and perfecter of our faith" (Hebrews 12:1-2).

The New Testament mentions five specific crowns believers can look forward to as eternal rewards. Two different words in the Greek language can be translated "crown." One of the words is *diadem* and refers to a king's crown; the other is *stephanos,* which refers to the crown given to an overcomer or to the winner of a race. In heaven, Jesus wears the *diadem* and believers receive the *stephanos.*

With that in mind, the five eternal rewards include the *crown of life* for those who are faithful in managing the trials and temptations of life (James 1:12), the *crown of glory* for Christian leaders who serve with humility and faithfulness (1 Peter 5:2-4), the *crown of rejoicing* for those that lead others to faith in Jesus (1 Thessalonians 2:19-20 KJV), the *crown of righteousness* for those that finish well and wait with longing for the return of Jesus Christ (2 Timothy 4:8), and the *imperishable crown* for those that exercise spiritual discipline and self-control in the Christian life. Because self-control is listed among the fruit of the Spirit in Galatians 5, the imperishable crown is probably for those that live the Spirit-filled life well.

These five crowns are the only specific rewards mentioned in the Bible, and it's worth noting that in eternity believers cast their crowns before the worthy One in a heavenly act of worship (Revelation 4:10-11). It's also reasonable to assume that God has other ways of rewarding faithful service to Him. In the Sermon on the Mount, Jesus said, "Beware of practicing your righteousness before other people in order to be seen by them, for then you will have no eternal reward from your Father who is in heaven" (Matthew 6:1). The specific acts of righteousness Jesus goes on to mention include giving, praying, and fasting, which appear to have their own reward in heaven.

How Are You Managing the Trust?

Third, because you will appear before the judgment seat of Christ, manage your life like a sacred trust. To the Romans, Paul writes,

> Why do you pass judgment on your brother? Or you, why do you despise your brother? For we will all stand before the judgment seat of God; for it is written, "As I live, says the Lord, every knee shall bow to me, and every tongue shall confess to God." So then each of us will give an account of himself to God (14:10-12).

The judgment seat of Christ has practical implications beyond the obvious. For example, the reality of this future judgment for believers should make us think twice about judging others, because "each of us will give an account of himself to God." This syncs with what Jesus famously said in the Sermon on the Mount about not judging others. With a twinge of Hebrew humor, He warned us not to waste time inspecting the speck of dust in someone else's eye when you have a log in your own eye. "For with the judgment you pronounce you will be judged" (Matthew 7:1-5).

Life is also a sacred trust. To illustrate this idea, Jesus once told a story about an unfaithful steward that squandered his master's wealth. When the report came to the master about the mismanagement of his possessions, he called the manager into his office and said, "What is this I hear about you? Turn in the account of your management, for you can no longer be manager" (Luke 16:1-2). The parable goes on to say how the unfaithful steward acted shrewdly by summoning his master's debtors and cutting financial deals with them. With a view to eternity, Jesus then applies the following stewardship principles,

> "One who is faithful in a very little is also faithful in much, and one who is dishonest in a very little is also dishonest in much. If then you have not been faithful in the unrighteous wealth, who will entrust to you the true riches? And if you have not been faithful in that which is another's, who will give you that which is your own?" (Luke 16:10-12).

Stewardship 101 says God owns everything on earth and in heaven (Psalm 24:1; Haggai 2:8). We, on the other hand, are merely managers of someone else's wealth. As someone once quipped, "Money is tainted; 'taint yours and it 'taint mine." For that reason, every financial decision on earth is also a spiritual decision that impacts eternity. It might help you to imagine you're drawing upon God's bank account when you write a check or use your debit card. If you cannot faithfully manage the "unrighteous wealth" God entrusts to you on earth, why would He give you anything to manage for Him in heaven, or transfer any of His "true riches" to your ownership?

The implications of this parable in Luke 16 are stunning and should motivate each of us to immediately align our personal financial management to biblical principles. The faithful management of earthly wealth involves earning, giving, saving, investing, and spending money (hopefully in that order) with the future judgment seat of Christ in view because, like the steward in the parable, "each of us will give an account of himself to God."

Does any of this make you nervous? As a believer in Jesus Christ, consider the judgment seat of Christ a gentle wake-up call. Are you concerned that you could experience sadness, shame, and a sense of personal loss when heaven opens the accounting books on the management of your life? First John 2:28 does warn, "And now, little children, abide in him, so that when he appears we may have confidence and not shrink from him in shame at his coming," and 2 John 8 says, "Watch yourselves, so that you may not lose what [you] have worked for, but may win a full reward." These are fair warnings from Scripture that we should heed. They remind me of how I encourage my kids to study hard in school because the rewards of a good job and career go to those who prepare academically.

With academics in mind, Herman Hoyt compares the judgment seat of Christ for believers to a commencement ceremony. He says at a high school graduation, for example, "there is some measure of disappointment and remorse that one did not do better and work harder. However, at such an event, the overwhelming emotion is joy, not remorse."[65] This is a great way to think about the believer's day of reward. Everyone graduates and receives a diploma; some graduate with honors; some just graduate.

So, I ask you again, how are you building your life? How are you running the race? How are you managing the trust? Soon we must all appear before the judgment seat of Christ.

22

Angels Watching Over Us

No study of the afterlife would be complete without mentioning angels. If culture is any indication, the "heavenly host" is of great interest to us. Disney, for example, popularized angels in a 1994 movie by putting them in the outfield of a baseball game. The producers were inspired by a Major League Baseball team in Anaheim near Los Angeles, the city of angels, called the California Angels. Oprah has her "Angel Network" and regularly mixes a discussion of angels into her parade of guests who promote New Age mysticism. *Touched by an Angel* was one of the most popular television shows in Hollywood history. And if you consider all the angelic jewelry, figurines, and collectibles available, you get the sense that angels are everywhere. Indeed, many people believe they are watching over us.

Years ago when contemporary Christian music was emerging as a pop genre, Amy Grant hit the charts with a song titled "Angels Watching Over Me." The GRAMMY award-winning performer tapped into the curiosity many of us possess toward these magnificent celestial beings we read about in the Bible. The song begins by referencing the apostle Peter's miraculous release from prison by an angel who made the chains that bound him open up and fall to the ground. The song quickly turns to our present-day experiences with angels with the conclusion that angels are indeed watching over us all the time.

It's true that there's nothing more comforting than knowing your guardian angel (if there is such a thing) is there when you need him or her or it. Do the angels of heaven really watch over us? Are they sent to protect us, even fight for us when necessary? Who or what are these mysterious beings from heaven evangelist Billy Graham called "God's secret agents"? Are angels even real?

According to a 2011 poll conducted by the Associated Press, 77 percent of adults believe angels are real, including four in ten people who never attend religious services.[66] Trends also show that the more secularized American culture becomes, belief in beings like angels is paradoxically on the rise.[67] As popular as angels are today, we need to remember that revelation, not speculation, leads us to a true understanding of these heavenly beings. In other words, what God has revealed about angels in the Bible is fascinating enough.

"AND THEY WERE CREATED"

Let's start at the beginning, actually some time before the time when the Bible says "in the beginning, God created the heavens and the earth" (Genesis 1:1). Angels are created beings and there's ample evidence in Scripture to suggest that they were already in existence before God spoke the first words of creation recorded in the Bible's first chapter. For starters, Psalm 148:2-5 says, "Praise him, all his angels; praise him, all his hosts! Praise him, sun and moon, praise him, all you shining stars! Praise him, you highest heavens, and you waters above the heavens! Let them praise the name of the LORD! For he commanded and they were created."

Rewind that last sentence. "For he commanded and they were created." That includes the angels who praise Him. The New Testament confirms this fact when the apostle Paul writes of Christ, "For by him all things were created, in heaven and on earth, visible and invisible, whether thrones or dominions or rulers or authorities—all things were created through him and for him." Not only does Colossians 1:16 refute the teaching that Jesus Christ is a created being (an archangel—the highest of created beings—according to Jehovah's Witnesses), but from it we learn that He created everything seen and unseen, including the angelic hosts. Evidently, the angels are organized according to a command structure made up of "thrones," "dominions," "rulers," and "authorities." Nehemiah 9:6 also makes reference to angels ("the host of heaven") being created by God for the purpose of worshipping Him,

> "You are the Lord, you alone. You have made heaven, the heaven of heavens, with all their host, the earth and all that is on it, the seas and all that is in them; and you preserve all of them; and the host of heaven worships you."

So, when did God create the angels? The best we can surmise is at least one minute, probably more, before the account of creation in Genesis. I say that because when the Lord broke His silence with Job, He asked, "Where were you when I laid the foundation of the earth?" and then He adds this poetic reference to the angels, "when the morning stars sang together and all the sons of God shouted for joy?" (Job 38:4-7). From this we understand that the angels were present at the moment of creation, singing the praises of God and shouting for joy with more heartfelt expression than a stadium packed with euphoric college football fans on a Saturday afternoon. However, how much time elapsed between the creation of the "morning stars" and the first flash of light in Genesis chapter 1 is anyone's guess.

Ministering Spirits

At this point you might be wondering if any of this matters even slightly more than the answer to the age-old question about how many angels can dance on the head of a pin. The answer is yes, it does matter and much more than anybody's pinhead theory.

The order of creation matters as we consider our own origin, purpose, and eternal destiny in direct relation to the person and nature of Jesus. To this point, the writer of Hebrews goes to great lengths to establish the superiority of Jesus Christ as compared to the angels of heaven. Read these words slowly and carefully,

> After making purification for sins, he sat down at the right

> hand of the Majesty on high, having become as much superior to angels as the name he has inherited is more excellent than theirs. For to which of the angels did God ever say, "You are my Son, today I have begotten you"? Or again, "I will be to him a father, and he shall be to me a son"? And again, when he brings the firstborn into the world, he says, "Let all God's angels worship him." Of the angels he says, "He makes his angels winds, and his ministers a flame of fire." But of the Son he says, "Your throne, O God, is forever and ever, the scepter of uprightness is the scepter of your kingdom...And to which of the angels has he ever said, "Sit at my right hand until I make your enemies a footstool for your feet"? Are they not all ministering spirits sent out to serve for the sake of those who are to inherit salvation? (Hebrews 1:3-14).

The Bible places Jesus in a category all by Himself. He is not a created being, nor an archangel, nor the spirit brother of Lucifer as the Mormons teach. He is the one and only Son of God, co-equal with the Father and the Holy Spirit. As the late Bible scholar Zane Hodges says of Jesus, "He has attained an eminence far beyond anything the angels can claim."[68] If nothing else, this passage from Hebrews tells us that Jesus is far more deserving of our worship than the angels no matter how enthralled we are with them. In fact, nowhere in Scripture are we encouraged to worship angels. On the contrary, angels in the Bible regularly refuse such adulation from humans (Revelation 19:10).

The writer of Hebrews calls the angels "ministering spirits." Would it surprise you to know that they are sent by God to serve us? What an amazing and humbling idea! It reminds me of the time the psalmist made the following observation about God's work in creation:

> When I consider Your heavens, the work of Your fingers, the moon and the stars, which You have ordained, what is man that You are mindful of him, and the son of man that You visit him? For You have made him a little lower than the angels, and You have crowned him with glory and honor (Psalm 8:3-5 NKJV).

God created humans "a little lower than the angels" and then in a twist of irony sent the angels to serve us. Then, when God became a man in the person of Jesus Christ, the angels had two good reasons to serve Him—Jesus was fully God and fully human at the same time. The writer of Hebrews borrows the ancient writ from Psalm 8 and applies it to Jesus by saying, "You made him for a little while lower than the angels" (2:7). This speaks of the brief season Jesus lived on this earth as flesh and blood, during which time angels sang at His birth and ministered to Him after being tempted by the devil in the wilderness (Luke 2:14; Matthew 4:11).

Because of the way angels minister to humans, the writer of Hebrews also encourages us with these eye-popping words, "Do not neglect to show hospitality to strangers, for thereby some have entertained angels unawares" (13:2). This has led many to believe that angels can actually take on human form. If this is true (and I believe it is), it should at least make us think twice about how we treat strangers. The word "unawares" suggests we may never actually know when we're staring an angel in the face. We can only wonder.

In his book *Angels: God's Secret Agents,* Billy Graham makes us wonder by telling the story about a celebrated Philadelphia neurologist named Dr. S.W. Mitchell who was awakened one night by someone knocking on his door. It was a poorly dressed little girl who was deeply upset. Her mother was very ill and she begged the good doctor to come see her. It was a cold, snowy night in the city of brotherly love, but the weary medical doctor obliged. Graham writes,

> As *Reader's Digest* reports the story, he found the mother desperately ill with pneumonia. After arranging for medical care, he complimented the sick woman on the intelligence and persistence of her little daughter. The woman looked at him strangely and then said, "My daughter died a month ago." She added, "Her shoes and coat are in the clothes closet there." Dr. Mitchell, amazed and perplexed, went to the closet and opened the door. There hung the very coat worn by the little girl who had brought him to tend to her mother. It was warm and dry and could not possibly have been out in the wintry night.[69]

Graham then asks, "Was this the work of God's angels on behalf of the sick woman?" The Bible certainly leaves open that possibility, but in this life we may never know for sure. Again, we can only wonder.

CURIOUS BEINGS

Angels are curious beings who look into the affairs of humans. We might say they watch and collect data on us with as much interest as big brother government, but for different reasons.

For example, in his first letter to the Corinthians, the apostle Paul says he and the other apostles had become "a spectacle to the world, to angels and to men." Apparently, the angels of heaven are curious about the work we do, even when we serve as "fools for Christ's sake" (1 Corinthians 4:10). Peter adds to the mystery by saying salvation is something "into which angels long to look" (1 Peter 1:12). The particular Greek word the leather-faced fisherman uses means to stretch forward the head in order to get a better look. Angels don't participate in redemption, but they lean into our lives marked by God's grace with a curiosity greater than a monkey named George. Furthermore, angels are so excited when they see God's grace transform a human life, they actually throw a party in heaven (Luke 15:10).

Angels also watch the way we do church. In his letter to the Ephesians, Paul waxes eloquently about the wisdom of God manifested through the church of Jesus Christ. He says a grace was given to him "to preach to the Gentiles the unsearchable riches of Christ, and to bring to light for everyone what is the plan of the mystery hidden for ages in God who created all things" (Ephesians 3:8-9). I know, I know. That's heady stuff! Then Paul adds, "So that through the church the manifold wisdom of God might now be made known to the rulers and authorities in the heavenly places" (v. 10). Reading this makes my mind feel like I just orbited the Milky Way! Let's see if we can bring Paul's thoughts a little closer to earth.

The word "manifold" means multicolored and is rarely used in the New Testament. The late Bible teacher Ray Stedman says this word suggests that the wisdom and love of God are "manifest in all the hues of life—in our golden moments of glory, our green pastures of contentment, our red hours of anger and passion, our blue days of depression, our black days of grief. His many colors of wisdom are all aspects of his character. We cannot always see the full rainbow of his wisdom and love toward us, but it is there."[70]

Think about it. Through the church, God puts His rainbow-like wisdom on display, but to whom? According to Paul, God showcases His character "to the rulers and authorities in the heavenly places." This refers to the angels and probably the demons too. Picture in your sanctified imagination an invisible spiritual kingdom made up of both faithful and fallen angels. They watch us and learn from us. They are the audience and we are the actors in a cosmic theater where God is both the director and the executive producer. Ray Stedman explores this fascination further when he writes,

> As the angels watch us, they see us learning to turn from our fears, anger and sin, as we learn to trust God. When the angels, who have seen God, see that weak and faltering humans, who have never seen God, can learn to trust and obey Him, they cannot help but praise Him...When the angels—especially the fallen angels of [hell]—see that frail humans succeed where angels failed, loving and obeying the same God that demons rebelled against, then the true wisdom and righteousness of God is demonstrated for all time.[71]

What's happening in the unseen heavenly realms is just as real as what we see with the naked eye. Knowing that we play a part in showcasing God's eternal wisdom to the "rulers and authorities in the heavenly places" should also motivate every follower of Jesus to live the Christian life authentically, and do church well by putting aside our petty differences in the body of Christ.

My Own Brush with Angels

My own brush with angels watching over me still runs chills up and down my spine. I close this chapter with one of two personal stories that make me wonder if I once, maybe twice, entertained angels without realizing it. The first story relates to the first time I ever stood in the pulpit of a church. I was a teenager and had won a Scripture memory contest that my youth pastor used to challenge us to grow in our relationship with God. One passage of Scripture I recalled from memory was all twenty-four verses of Psalm 139. I did so with the help of my mother who listened to my practice recitations after dinner each night. To this day, Psalm 139 is one of my favorites.

My youth pastor was impressed with all that I had put to memory during the discipleship challenge. He asked me to recite Psalm 139 from memory before the entire congregation on Youth Night. I agreed and a few weeks later found myself standing behind the wooden pulpit in the chapel of our church wearing a brown leisure suit and staring at approximately three hundred people. I don't know which was worse—the nervous adrenalin racing through my veins or the mod, shirt-like jacket I wore with matching bell-bottoms. It was an overflow crowd for a Sunday night, and I was terrified! I thought, *What if my mind freezes like a polar ice cap and I can't get the first words past my lips?*

My family arrived early to get a good seat not far from the front. People packed in pews shoulder-to-shoulder on the main floor and in the small balcony. Some even stood in the back of the auditorium. Youth Night was always popular at our northern Indiana church, but something in the air made this night feel special.

The time came for me to recite the verses and all went well. My mind clicked and the words flowed easily out of my heart and mouth. I felt the rush of the Holy Spirit flow through me like living water. I missed a small phrase around verse 16 but hardly anyone noticed except the Holy Ghost and my mother. Afterward, I sat down and listened intently as my youth pastor delivered a challenging message to teens from Joshua 1. As the service ended and people began filing out of the auditorium, my older brother turned to my mother and said, "Where did they go?"

"Where did who go?" she replied.

"Those two people who were sitting next to us. Where are they?"

Apparently, two people my family had never seen before sat nearby.

Because the church was growing with a steady stream of visitors every week, it wasn't unusual to see new people. What was unusual was how the two strangers disappeared so quickly. Where did they go was a reasonable question given the gridlock in the aisles.

Picture in your mind a small, traditional chapel with a middle aisle, pews on both sides, and double doors at the back of the room. After the pastor gave the benediction, people began emptying out of the pews and into the middle and outer aisles, but movement was slow due to the larger-than-usual crowd. After only a few moments, the two visitors disappeared. We turned to talk to them, but they were gone. We looked again to the left and to the right, but they were nowhere to be found. My brother insisted they literally had to leap over the pews to get out of the chapel before everyone else, but that was unlikely. Were they angels watching over a future preacher of the gospel? Who knows? We all agreed there was rare air in the room that night. And it was around that time I first sensed God was calling me into the ministry. To this day we can only speculate about the possibility of a host of angelic beings, seen and unseen, filling the small chapel.

Angels watch over us in other ways too. Some say we each have a guardian angel to protect us from harm and to fight our spiritual battles. Is this true? The Bible is still the best source of information about such things, not Hollywood. So, let's take a closer look at these mysterious heavenly creatures called angels.

23

Angels in the Realms of Glory and Beyond

To thousands of people in cities all across the United States, Curtis Sliwa is an angel. The former night manager at McDonald's is the founder of a citizen brigade that began in New York City on February 13, 1979. Sliwa used his co-workers at the Fordham Road fast-food restaurant to form voluntary patrol units that went into notorious inner-city neighborhoods to board up buildings and clean up bombed-out vacant lots. Without weapons to protect themselves and others, they also rode the subway between the toughest stops, looking for gang members that had committed crimes and detaining them until police arrived. Though many officials were initially suspicious of the red-beret-wearing vigilantes, their city streets became safer thanks to a group that became known as The Guardian Angels.

The Guardian Angels is a fitting name for the volunteer safety and protection organization recognized by presidents, cheered by mayors, and endorsed by business, entertainment, and urban leaders worldwide.[72] Of course, the name comes from the biblical notion that we each have a real guardian angel dispatched from heaven to watch over us.

Is this true? What does the Bible says about angels that guard us?

Matthew 18:10 is a good place to begin this discussion. To illustrate a point about the Father's concern for even one sheep that goes astray, Jesus drew a small child near to Him and said to His disciples, "See that you do not despise one of these little ones. For I tell you that in heaven their angels always see the face of my Father who is in heaven." It's from this statement that some argue the point about guardian angels. However, the most we can say is that angels guard God's "little ones" in a collective sense. It's a stretch to suggest that God assigns a specific angel to protect each believer in Jesus, let alone every child. But don't let that discourage you from finding comfort in the idea that angels really do watch over us in a protective way. Even the devil knows the angels stand guard over God's children. Psalm 91:9-12 says,

> Because you have made the LORD your dwelling place—the Most High, who is my refuge—no evil shall be allowed to befall you, no plague come near your tent. For he will command his angels concerning you to guard you in all your ways. On their hands they will bear you up, lest you strike your foot against the stone.

This is the passage the devil quoted when he tempted Jesus to catapult Himself from the top of the temple. The serpent of old knows the Bible well enough to play cunningly with the words God speaks just as he did with Eve in the Garden of Eden. He uses holy writ to his own advantage, intentionally twisting God's word to deceive us. To this point, the devil said to Jesus, "If you are the Son of God, throw yourself down, for it is written, 'He will command his angels concerning you,' and 'on their hands they will bear you up, lest you strike your foot against the stone'" (Matthew 4:5-6).

Read it again, this time carefully comparing it to the Old Testament version. Did you notice how the devil conveniently left out the phrase "to guard you in all your ways"? Did he really think he could pull the shades down over Jesus's eyes?

Bible commentator James Montgomery Boice notes how the phrase "in all your ways" refers to "the ways marked out for us by God and not our own willful ways."[73] It's clear that the devil tempted Jesus to go his own way rather than the way of the cross the Father willed for

Him. Fortunately Jesus saw through the devil's scheme and fired back from Scripture saying, "Again it is written, 'You shall not put the Lord your God to the test'" (Matthew 4:7). Score one for Jesus.

The point is we presume on the Lord when we go our own way and still expect Him to send His angels to keep us from smashing our lives into a hundred broken pieces. The promise of angelic protection is always conditioned upon us going God's way. The psalmist assumes we've made the Lord our "dwelling place." In other words, if we make something or someone else our place of refuge, we step out from under God's protection plan. Because Jesus always chose to trust His heavenly Father, the angels were always nearby. After the wilderness temptation, the Bible says, "Then the devil left him, and behold, angels came and were ministering to him" (Matthew 4:11).

If the angels of heaven do stand guard over us, why do bad things happen to God's people even when we are doing our best to walk in the ways our heavenly Father has marked out for us? Some say because God is powerless to protect His children. He wants to deliver us from evil, but He is limited and unable to do so. I find that answer unsatisfactory and unbiblical. However, the perfect answer to the nagging question will have to wait until we enter the hereafter.

For His own sovereign reasons that He's under no obligation to explain, the most powerful Being in the universe allows us to live in a fallen and dangerous world where, for a time, evil things befall good people, even the youngest and most vulnerable among us. Because the Bible says "some have entertained angels unawares" (Hebrews 13:2), it follows that angels have surely engaged their protective services unawares. For every time we wonder why an angel didn't guard us or a child from harm, we need to consider that perhaps one did without our notice more times than we can count. Jesus acknowledged the reality of evil in the world and then sternly warned, "Woe to the one by whom the temptation comes!" (Matthew 18:7). I take His warning to mean justice will prevail in eternity.

Neither of these passages from the Bible (Matthew 18; Psalm 91) teaches unequivocally that individual angels are assigned to guard individual believers. But know this for sure: collectively, the angels of heaven stand ready to come to our rescue when we run into trouble as we live out God's will for our lives. Jesus said the angels "always see the face of my Father in heaven." I take this to mean they never turn their eyes away from the Father so as not to miss an opportunity—perhaps a direct order—to spring into action on our behalf.

I remember one time when it must have been an angel that protected me and other drivers on the Dallas freeway from severe, even fatal, injury. Years ago while on a business trip to the Lone Star state, I rented a car and crisscrossed the city while selling medical supplies to my customers. I was young, a recent college graduate, and unfamiliar with the city and its heavy traffic. While merging into a busy lane from an on-ramp, I got tangled up with an eighteen-wheel truck. As I pulled out, he couldn't slow down enough to avoid clipping the back end of my car. At nearly sixty-miles-per-hour, I spun across four lanes of traffic and into the grassy knoll between the two sides of the multilane freeway. To make matters worse, it happened during the afternoon rush hour, which meant a wreckage of shocked and angry motorists piled up behind me.

I sat in my car for a few moments, caught my breath, and realized I was okay. Not a scrape, cut, or bruise on my body. My heart was just racing as fast as a NASCAR chase at the nearby Texas Motor Speedway. A few minutes later, rescue vehicles arrived in force including police, fire trucks, and ambulances with red and blue flashing lights. Chevy and Ford trucks were scattered everywhere. Remember, this was Texas! It was one of those scenes that backed up traffic for miles and miles and even became the lead story on the six o'clock news.

It took more than an hour for rescue personnel to sort things out. The police officer had been working his way up from the back of the accident, interviewing victims to determine what actually happened, when he finally reached me. Dressed like a Texas county mountie with his pants tucked into his leather boots and wearing a pair of Ray-Ban sunglasses, the bald-headed traffic cop was chuckling as he approached me. Yes, chuckling! I failed to see the humor in the situation as he assured me nobody had been injured in the multicar pileup. He just couldn't figure out what triggered the crash. When I explained what happened between the trucker and me, the officer laughed again, shook his head, and said, "There must have been an angel dancing on the hood of your car." I agreed.

Glimpses of Glory

From the realms of glory God dispatches His angels to guard over us. John MacArthur notes, "Study the Bible and you will find angels in the third heaven, where God dwells. There they worship Him continually. You'll find them in the second heaven, traversing the universe, serving God in various ways. And you'll find them in the first heaven, even intervening from time to time in human affairs."[74] Let's take a closer look at the heavenly host as they do what they do best: worship the living God of heaven and earth.

The book of Revelation gives us several glimpses into the glory of heaven and the angelic host that surrounds the throne of God. In his book *All the Angels of the Bible,* Herbert Lockyer calls the Apocalypse of Jesus Christ "the angel book of the New Testament" for its many references to these beautiful and mysterious creatures.[75]

For example, an angel from heaven appeared to the apostle John and gave him the vision of end times (1:1-2). Angels also fight spiritual wars (12:7-12), support the preaching of the gospel (14:6-7), assist the servants of God on earth (7:2-3), and deliver destruction through a series of seal, bowl, and trumpet judgments. An angel of the Lord even locks up Satan for a thousand years in the bottomless pit during the Millennium (20:1-2). Mostly, the angels worship God in the realms of glory.

John's first glimpse of untainted worship comes in chapter 4 where he sees twenty-four elders and four living creatures surrounding the heavenly throne, enveloped by stunning beauty and majesty. John says He who sits on the throne "had the appearance of jasper and carnelian, and around the throne was a rainbow that had the appearance of an emerald" (4:3). No wonder the twenty-four elders, a representation of the church, fall down and worship Him who lives forever. Revelation 5:11-14 adds a multitude of angels to the thrilling worship scene.

> Then I looked, and I heard around the throne and the living creatures and the elders the voice of many angels, numbering myriads of myriads and thousands of thousands, saying with a loud voice, "Worthy is the Lamb who was slain, to receive power and wealth and wisdom and might and honor and glory and blessing!" And I heard every creature in heaven and on earth and under the earth and in the sea, and all that is in them, saying, "To him who sits on the throne and to the Lamb be blessing and honor and glory and might forever and ever!" And the four living creatures said, "Amen!" and the elders fell down and worshiped.

Imagine a choir with "myriads of myriads, and thousands of thousands" of angelic voices praising the Lamb of God who alone is worthy of worship. How many angels are we talking about? At a minimum, one thousand times one thousand equals one million. But John uses plurals, myriads and thousands, so the number could be infinite. Whatever the number is, by comparison, the Mormon Tabernacle Choir with its four hundred voices will look like a men's quartet.

As we might expect, singing will be a huge part of our worship experience in heaven. The good news is our voices will join in perfect harmony with the angels. For a guy like me that cannot carry a tune across the street, this is really good news. For once I get to do more than merely make a joyful noise, or in my case a joyful screech. Every voice in the heavenly choir, including mine, will sound forth with perfect pitch. And there will be no worship wars in heaven; nobody will complain about the style of music or that the music is too loud. Even though John notes how they all sang with a "loud voice," I suspect it's the kind of loudness that will neither hurt our ears nor disturb the worshipful reflection in our hearts. Lyrics matter in heaven too, as evidenced by these words recorded in the Apocalypse of Jesus:

> They cast their crowns before the throne, saying, "Worthy are you, our Lord and God, to receive glory and honor and power, for you created all things, and by your will they existed and were created" (Revelation 4:10-11).

> And they sang a new song, saying, "Worthy are you to take the scroll and to open its seals, for you were slain, and by your blood you ransomed people for God from every tribe and language and people and nation, and you have made them a kingdom and priests to our God, and they shall reign on the earth" (Revelation 5:9-10).

Heaven is full of exhilarating worship with theological soundness and laser-like focus on the One who redeemed us by His own blood. Multiethnicity also characterizes the experience and place where God dwells with every tribe, language, people, and nation. Eleven o'clock on Sunday morning might still be the most segregated hour of the week in many churches across America, but it won't be that way in heaven. The song lyrics I referenced also mention creation twice. Throughout eternity we will sing about how we were created and exist according to God's will and intention. No wonder the creation story in the Bible's book of Genesis is still one of the most attacked and maligned aspects of the Christian faith.

With so much worship directed to the Lamb who sits on the throne, it shouldn't surprise us to find angels warning humans not to worship angels (Revelation 19:10; 22:8-9). Lockyer says, "The tendency to be blinded by the angel rather than enlightened by its message is an ever-present threat."[76]

In the order of creation, angels are special creatures but never more special than Jesus who is their Creator too (Colossians 1:16). We should always remember that though Jesus was made "lower than the angels" for "a little while" (a reference to His incarnation), today the Savior holds the most superior name and position found anywhere in the universe. As the writer of Hebrews asks, "For to which of the angels did God ever say, 'You are my Son, today I have begotten you'?" (Hebrews 1:5).

24

Eternity for Those Who Can't Believe

Jacob's life on earth began prematurely, only twenty-two weeks after his loving parents conceived him. "The feisty one" lived for exactly two months, even though doctors thought he would either die at birth or enter this world severely handicapped. My friends Deane and Linda, the proud grandparents and members of the church we served in Washington DC, prayed for baby Jacob with tears every day and night. Moreover, we joined with them and hundreds of others across the United States, earnestly seeking the Great Physician on behalf of the precious child.

From our limited human perspective, Jacob came into this world too soon and departed too early. In His infinite wisdom, God knew from the beginning that Jacob would not live a long life on earth, which, in the hearts of most compassionate people, raises the question: "Why, God?"

Though we may never receive an answer to the why question, we can (and must) trust that our sovereign God and heavenly Father is too good to be unkind and too wise to make a mistake. But the news of Jacob's death brought yet another question: *Where is Jacob now?*

Is he in heaven? Like you, I can't imagine a loving God would condemn an infant child to hell who can't respond in faith to the gospel. But that's not a good enough reason to believe Jacob is in heaven today. We must jettison sentimentality from this discussion and replace it with sound biblical theology. That said, the Bible gives us good reasons to indeed believe Jacob is in heaven.

WHEN CAN A CHILD BELIEVE?

Generally, those who can't believe (due to lack of opportunity to hear or comprehend) include aborted fetuses, stillborn children, infants, young children, and those born with intellectual disabilities.

We know that every child is a gift from God who never makes a mistake (Psalm 127), although one of the great mysteries of life is how God is glorified through a child's suffering and through the heartache of heroic parents who care for those who can't believe. While it's true that some mentally challenged souls are capable of much more than we think they are, and are thus responsible for their own beliefs, many others are totally incapable of understanding and believing in the gospel.

So, exactly when is a child responsible for his or her own beliefs? At what age is what some Bible scholars call the "age of accountability?" In other words, at what age is belief in Jesus Christ for salvation possible?

Let's review what the Bible teaches about the human condition, why we need salvation, and what God says about the only way to obtain a right relationship with Him. Romans 3:23 tells us, "All have sinned and fall short of the glory of God." The "glory of God" is His moral perfection and absolute standard of holiness. Everyone falls way short of that standard. This means all of us are in the same lousy spiritual condition—fallen, depraved, out of favor with God, and enemies of the Almighty. Yes, enemies!

Thankfully two chapters later, the apostle Paul adds, "For if while we were enemies we were reconciled to God by the death of his Son" (Romans 5:10). It is indeed good news to hear the gospel of Jesus Christ after hearing that diagnosis of our human condition.

From the inspired pen of King David, the Bible furthermore teaches that we were conceived in iniquity (Psalm 51:5). Bible scholars refer to this as original sin. The idea is that we inherited a sin nature from our parents who got it from their parents and so on all the way back to our forefather Adam who, with his wife Eve, disobeyed God (Genesis 3). The Bible says "one trespass led to condemnation for all men" and "by the one man's disobedience the many were made sinners" (Romans 5:18-19).

You think that doesn't sound fair?

Fair or not, sin is like a computer virus that has corrupted the entire human operating system.

If you have any doubts about the systemic nature of sin, just look around at our crazy world, or honestly look inside your own self. Can you really disagree with the Bible's diagnosis of the human heart as being "deceitful above all things, and desperately sick" (Jeremiah 17:9)?

Thus, we sin because we are sinners by nature. In addition, Bible scholars make another important distinction between original sin and actual sins. A newborn baby inherits a sin nature in the same way everyone else does at the moment of conception, but that child does not commit actual sins for which God holds him accountable until he or she understands the difference between right and wrong. James 4:17 alludes to this by saying, "So whoever knows the right thing to do and fails to do it, for him it is sin." So, when does a child know right from wrong? When can a child believe? The answer to that question varies from child to child based on the age of accountability.

The age at which a child grasps the gospel is not the same for everyone. My son made a true profession of faith in kindergarten. I know that because I have seen his faith grow throughout his adolescent and teenage years. Months after he prayed to express his faith in Jesus, he challenged me by asking, "Daddy, why won't you baptize me!" He saw me baptizing others and wanted to experience it for himself. I hadn't refused to baptize him; I merely thought he should wait until he understood what baptism meant for believers. However, he persisted and I had the joy of witnessing my little boy's public profession of faith by baptizing him in the name of the Father, the Son, and the Holy Spirit. My daughter, on the other hand, believed in Jesus later in her adolescent years.

Others throughout church history professed their faith in Christ at an early age, including Jonathan Edwards, Richard Baxter, and the well-known hymn-writer Isaac Watts. They trusted Jesus as their Savior at age eight, six, and nine respectively.[77] This does not make them super-saints. It just goes to show that all children do not understand and respond to the gospel at the same age.

A scene in the Old Testament gives us further insight into when a child can believe. The book of Deuteronomy records a series of messages Moses delivered to the generation of Israelites that came out of Egypt with him and wandered in the wilderness for forty years. At the edge of the Promised Land, Moses informed them that because of their stubborn rebellion, "not one of these men of this evil generation shall see the good land that I swore to give to your fathers."

This news devastated them! Even Moses died without taking possession of the land. However, the leather-faced leader assured them of these words from the Lord, who said, "As for your little ones, who you said would become a prey, and your children, who today have no knowledge of good or evil, they shall go in there. And to them I will give it, and they shall possess it" (Deuteronomy 1:34-40). The Hebrew children that had not reached the age of accountability ("no knowledge of good or evil") received a pass and entered the Promised Land based on the promise God made to Abraham, Isaac, and Jacob. With regard to heaven, does God do the same for those who can't believe? And if He does, on what basis does He do it? The answer is still by the finished work of Christ on the cross.

Is Jesus the Only Way for Those Who Can't Believe?

Dr. Robert Lightner, one of my professors at Dallas Theological Seminary or "Lightning Bob" as we affectionately called him, wrote a short but tender treatise called *Heaven for Those Who Can't Believe,* and I'm so grateful that he did. He argues that the finished work of Christ on the cross applies to those who can't believe because they haven't rejected the revelation of God.

> What of those who can't believe? My answer is, since the price has been paid in full, until it is rejected, the debt is cancelled. Therefore, God can receive into His presence all those who did not receive His Son by faith because they could not do so. Without violating His righteous demands in any way these are accepted into His presence. After all, His righteous demands were met at Calvary. The debt has been paid! Jesus paid it all![78]

This is glorious news for those who can't believe, and for parents and grandparents like Jacob's that have lost a child to death. Lightner goes on to say, "Christ's death paid the full price for the creature's sin. Until the Savior and His finished work are rejected, therefore, the debt remains cancelled."[79]

This raises another thorny question about the eternal destiny of those who have never heard the name of Jesus. What about the lost tribesman in New Guinea? Can the same argument be made for him or her? The answer is emphatically no. The eternal destiny of those who can't believe is not the same as those who have never heard the name of Jesus. Paul's letter to the Romans makes this clear.

> For the wrath of God is revealed from heaven against all ungodliness and unrighteousness of men, who by their unrighteousness suppress the truth. For what can be known about God is plain to them, because God has shown it to them. For his invisible attributes, namely, his eternal power and divine nature, have been clearly perceived, ever since the creation of the world, in the things that have been made. So they are without excuse (Romans 1:18-20).

The lost tribesman who is able to believe but has never heard the name of Jesus is still accountable for the revelation God gave in creation and in the human conscience. If the tribesman rejects natural revelation, he is then "without excuse." Most Bible teachers also believe that if he responds positively to natural revelation, God will see to it that he receives a more specific revelation of Himself. This has been proven over and over again through the work of missionary organizations all around the world. Lightner affirms this idea by saying,

> God reveals truth to an open heart. When men reject the lesser revelation of God in nature and conscience, they are demonstrating their rejection also of God's greater revelation in Christ...Response to God's message in nature and conscience does not bring salvation, but it does reveal a willingness to respond to God. It gives evidence of an open and receptive heart. When a person who lives in a land where the gospel is not heard and reaches the point where he can respond to God's revelation in nature and in his own conscience, he is no longer one who can't believe. At that point and from then on he is responsible for what he does with what he knows.[80]

And so, even for those who can't believe, the Bible still rings true about Jesus being the one and only way to heaven. The early apostles affirmed this about Jesus by saying, "And there is salvation in no one else, for there is no other name under heaven given among men by which we must be saved" (Acts 4:12; see also John 3:16; 14:6).

JESUS LOVES THE LITTLE CHILDREN

Another reason I believe Jacob and other children like him are in heaven is because of the way Jesus talked about and interacted with children. How Jesus loves the little children is a beautiful thing to behold in the Gospels. The Savior never married nor had biological children, which makes His sensitivity to young children even more impressive as a single adult. For me, marriage and fatherhood came in my early thirties. Until then, I was awkward around kids. I didn't go out of my way to notice them because I was too into me and my world. While some, including the disciples, thought children were a bother, Jesus always made time for them. Mark records one of the reasons we often sing "Jesus Loves the Little Children."

> And they were bringing children to him that he might

> touch them, and the disciples rebuked them. But when Jesus saw it, he was indignant and said to them, "Let the children come to me; do not hinder them, for to such belongs the kingdom of God. Truly, I say to you, whoever does not receive the kingdom of God like a child shall not enter it." And he took them in his arms and blessed them, laying his hands on them (Mark 10:13-16).

Jewish parents in the first century often brought their small children to a rabbi to receive his blessing by the laying on of hands. The disciples, however, bristled when this happened and their reaction disappointed Jesus. He used the opportunity to teach them an important spiritual lesson about His love for the little children. Jesus also knew something about them that the disciples didn't: children give us a glimpse inside the kingdom of God. This is true for two reasons. First, children have an amazing capacity for faith. For a child, seeing is not believing; believing is seeing. By embracing the little children the way He did, Jesus made it clear that a childlike faith is required for entrance into the kingdom of heaven. There are no skeptics in heaven, only former skeptics who became like little children.

Another reason children give us a glimpse inside the kingdom of heaven is because those who can't believe are welcome there. In two parallel passages that show the interaction of Jesus with children, the Savior noted how these little ones "believe in me" (Matthew 18:6; Mark 9:42). Lightner doubts the "little ones" Jesus was talking about were old enough to make a conscious decision about following Him. It's possible, however, that Jesus includes them as citizens of the kingdom of heaven because they had not reached an age where they could reject the revelation of God.

By the way, Jesus never assures the eternal destiny of those who can't believe because they were baptized or dedicated to God as an infant. The Bible identifies faith heroes like Samuel, Jeremiah, and John the Baptist as chosen or sanctified in the womb (1 Samuel 1:8–2:21; Jeremiah 1:5; Luke 1:15).[81] Not one of them was baptized as a baby. Furthermore, the practice of infant baptism gained popularity around A.D.

200 and in time developed as a tradition, identifying a child with the covenant community in the same way circumcision did in the Old Testament. However, nowhere does the New Testament encourage the baptizing of babies for that reason or any other, nor is baptism necessary for salvation (Ephesians 2:8-9). Rather, as an ordinance of the church, baptism is an act of obedience to Jesus's command and a way for those who have already believed in Him to make public their profession of faith (Matthew 28:19).

THE KING'S BABY BOY WHO COULD NOT BELIEVE

A final reason those who can't believe are in heaven lies in a story tucked away in the Old Testament. Nearly three thousand years before Jacob was born in Northern Virginia, an unexpected child arrived to an ancient king and his mistress in the Middle East. The Bible's second book of Samuel records the notorious liaison between David and Bathsheba. The eleventh chapter begins with an ominous tone, "In the spring of the year, the time when kings go out to battle...David remained at Jerusalem." The king's mistake? He stayed home when he was supposed to be on the battlefield. That's when his idle eyes wandered upon a bathing beauty. Lust seized David's heart and he misused his powers to fulfill his out-of-control desire.

My concern here is not so much with the sordid details that led to adultery and murder, or with how to affair-proof your marriage, but with the death of the child that resulted from the affair. The prophet Nathan confronted David with his sin and the king eventually repented in godly sorrow (Psalm 32 and 51). Afterward Nathan said, "Nevertheless, because by this deed you have utterly scorned the LORD, the child who is born to you shall die" (2 Samuel 12:14). In the very next verse, the Bible records these haunting words, "And the Lord afflicted the child that Uriah's wife bore to David, and he became sick." The nameless child died on his seventh day of life.

From our limited perspective, it seems cruel the Lord did such a thing. And it would be wrong for us to conclude that the death or disability of every child results from some sin in the parents' life. The disciples made this assumption about a man born blind and Jesus corrected their mistaken theology (John 9:1-7). What's different is that David was Israel's king and thus shouldered unique responsibilities to lead the covenant community. To whom much is given much is required. Therefore, David and Bathsheba's child expired before he would have been circumcised on the eighth day, forever marking him as a member of the covenant community. The Almighty's chastisement was in proportional response to the way David "scorned the Lord." But what did this mean about the child's eternal destiny? Did he die without the assurance of God's favor? He was certainly too young to know the difference between right and wrong. So where is the king's child who died before he could believe?

David spent the few days of his child's life fasting and praying, hoping beyond hope that the gracious Lord would change His mind and the child would live. But the Lord had spoken. David's prayers and humiliation could not alter heaven's decree, and the child died as prophesied.

In one sense, it must have been reassuring for David to know that the divine word spoken through the prophet Nathan was trustworthy. Perhaps this explains his actions after he learned of the child's fate. The king mystified his servants when he "arose from the earth and washed and anointed himself and changed his clothes" (v. 20). Instead of properly mourning in ashes and dust, David worshipped the Lord. He then broke his fast and when his servants asked, "What is this thing that you have done?" David said these memorable words,

> "While the child was still alive, I fasted and wept, for I said, 'Who knows whether the Lord will be gracious to me, that the child may live?' But now he is dead. Why should I fast? Can I bring him back again? I shall go to him, but he will not return to me" (2 Samuel 12:22-23).

It's worth noting that David did not pray for his dead child. His prayers for his sick baby boy stopped the moment he passed from this life into the next. That's when he turned his attention to the child's grieving mother (2 Samuel 12:24). Even more noteworthy is David's theology of the afterlife, though the subject of debate. My take is that he knew his child was with the Lord in heaven. It would have provided David little comfort if all he meant by "I shall go to him" was that one day he will be buried in the family tomb next to his child. The words "but he will not return to me" also suggest that his hope was not in reincarnation but in a future resurrection that he writes about in Psalm 16.

To sorrowing parents who have lost a child who could not believe, I say rest assured in the Lord's goodness and in the finished work of Christ on the cross. It's hard to imagine a grief on earth that is greater than the loss of a child. But as believers in Jesus Christ, we do not grieve as those who have no hope, and God promises to wipe away all of our tears (1 Thessalonians 4:13; Revelation 21:4). Until then, consider the words of author and teacher Vance Havner who said, "When you know where something is, you haven't lost it."

An Afterword About the Afterlife

The last book of the Bible records an eye-popping unveiling of Jesus Christ as received in a vision and penned by the apostle John while exiled on the Island of Patmos. As you read the first chapter of the book of Revelation, you'll catch a glimpse of Jesus perhaps as you've never seen Him before.

John says the Son of Man appeared to him wearing a long robe with a golden sash. His snow-white hair provided a sharp contrast to His eyes that burned like a flame of fire, and He spoke with a loud voice that sounded like the roar of a great waterfall. No wonder John fell to the ground like a dead man at the burnished bronze feet of Jesus. That's when the aging apostle heard these words,

> "Fear not, I am the first and the last, and the living one. I died, and behold I am alive forevermore, and I have the keys of Death and Hades" (Revelation 1:17-18).

The words "fear not" appear often in Scripture. To the person who is held in slavery by the fear of death, they evoke the sound of broken chains falling to the ground (Hebrews 2:15). These words and the picture of the glorified Jesus found in Revelation 1 should comfort anyone who dares to consider what happens after death. Jesus is alive forevermore! The Savior alone holds the keys to your eternal future and mine.

By now, having read the preceding chapters, I hope the afterlife isn't as mysterious to you as it once was. With the Word of God as our travel guide, we have gone to places that only divine revelation can take us. But the promise of heaven is only true for the person who believes on the Lord Jesus Christ.

You ask, "Why must I place my faith in Jesus Christ alone?"

Answer: Because He is "the living one."

He alone conquered sin and death. As I heard one Christ follower recently testify, "From all the religions, I chose the one with a God who is alive!" Furthermore, you need Jesus because, like me, you are unfit for heaven, having broken God's law. If you have any doubts about that, read the Ten Commandments, the righteous standard of God found in Exodus 20. I encourage you to go there right now and read the law that expresses God's perfect moral character, and then honestly evaluate your own life alongside it.

1. "You shall have no other gods before me.
2. "You shall not make for yourself a carved image, or any likeness of anything that is in heaven above, or that is in the earth beneath, or that is in the water under the earth. You shall not bow down to them or serve them, for I the LORD your God am a jealous God, visiting the iniquity of the fathers on the children to the third and the fourth generation of those who hate me, but showing steadfast love to thousands of those who love me and keep my commandments.
3. "You shall not take the name of the LORD your God in vain, for the LORD will not hold him guiltless who takes his name in vain.
4. "Remember the Sabbath day, to keep it holy. Six days you shall labor, and do all your work, but the seventh day is

a Sabbath to the LORD your God. On it you shall not do any work, you, or your son, or your daughter, your male servant, or your female servant, or your livestock, or the sojourner who is within your gates. For in six days the LORD made heaven and earth, the sea, and all that is in them, and rested on the seventh day. Therefore the LORD blessed the Sabbath day and made it holy.

5. "Honor your father and your mother, that your days may be long in the land that the LORD your God is giving you.
6. "You shall not murder.
7. "You shall not commit adultery.
8. "You shall not steal.
9. "You shall not bear false witness against your neighbor.
10. "You shall not covet your neighbor's house; you shall not covet your neighbor's wife, or his male servant, or his female servant, or his ox, or his donkey, or anything that is your neighbor's" (Exodus 20:3-17).

So, have you ever lied? Are you telling the truth right now? Have you ever stolen something that doesn't belong to you, even a little thing? When your neighbor comes home with a shiny new Corvette, do you wish you owned that car? That's called covetousness.

Have you ever used God's name as a cuss word?

Have you ever looked at another woman (or man) and imagined the sexual possibilities? That's called lust, and Jesus called lust adultery in the heart (Matthew 5:28).

We've only covered five of the Ten Commandments. How are you doing? Are you ready to admit to God you are a liar, a thief, a blasphemer, and an adulterer who is full of covetousness? The Bible summarizes our spiritual condition by saying, "All have sinned and fall short of the glory of God" (Romans 3:23). That news is bad enough and it gets worse before it gets better. The Bible goes on to say, "The wages of sin is death; but the gift of God is eternal life through Jesus

Christ our Lord" (Romans 6:23 KJV). A painful payday called death awaits all sinners! But God is generous and wants to give you eternal life. Honestly, after reading His Ten Commandments, which do you deserve, eternal life or eternal death?

Since you deserve eternal death because you have broken God's laws, how will things turn out for you on the Day of Judgment? Does God grade on a curve? Hardly. Will He look the other way and disregard the fact that you have trampled His commands? Don't count on that happening unless Somebody else steps in and pays the penalty for your sins. Well, that's exactly what Jesus did for you, and it's why the gospel is such good news. The Bible says, "For our sake he made him to be sin who knew no sin, so that in him we might become the righteousness of God" (2 Corinthians 5:21).

In other words, Jesus died *for* you; He died in your place. His death upon the cross paid in full the penalty you deserved for breaking God's commands. In this way, God is both just and loving at the same time. No verse of Scripture captures the essence of God's good news better than John 3:16, which reads, "For God so loved the world, that he gave his only Son, that whoever believes in him should not perish but have eternal life."

Elsewhere, the Bible says,

> For by grace you have been saved through faith. And this is not your own doing; it is the gift of God, not a result of works, so that no one may boast (Ephesians 2:8-9).

In Christianity, salvation is free of charge! Grace is God's way of giving you something you do not deserve. Grace is necessary because all of your best efforts to please God and earn His favor are like "filthy rags" (Isaiah 64:6 NIV). That's why the Protestant Reformers once rallied we are saved by grace alone *(sola gratia)* and by faith alone *(sola fide)*.

You are not saved *by* good works like trying your best to keep the Ten Commandments (you've already seen how futile that is), but you are saved *for* good works (Ephesians 2:10). Loving sacrifice and service to the One who gave His life for you is the proper response of your life to God's grace.

It cost Jesus everything to rescue you from the penalty and power of sin, and to provide you with an eternal home in heaven. He willingly shed His blood for you and then rose triumphantly from the grave. Before He returned to heaven, He promised to come again (John 14:3). In the meantime, He assured His followers, "I am with you always, to the very end of the age" (Matthew 28:20). Has anyone else done that for you? As a follower of Jesus named Peter said in a clarifying moment, "Lord, to whom shall we go? You have the words of eternal life, and we have believed, and have come to know, that you are the Holy One of God" (John 6:68-69). Does that describe the reality in your heart?

Religion is spelled D-O; Christianity is spelled D-O-N-E. It's all about what Jesus Christ has done for you.

There came a time in my life when I was finished with religion. I realized I could never be good enough to achieve God's standard of righteousness, and I was devastated to learn that He wasn't lowering the standard for me. I was weary and tired of trying and failing. Religion made me feel like I was taking a college entrance exam that required a perfect score and I kept falling short. Then I learned that Jesus took the exam for me. He kept the law of God perfectly and was willing to apply His score to my heavenly entrance application.

Is it really that easy? Yes, I remind you "the gift of God is eternal life through Jesus Christ our Lord" (Romans 6:23 KJV). The total salvation package, which includes a home in heaven, is a *gift* from God. Faith is the proper response to God's gracious offer, and the only one that pleases Him (Hebrews 11:6). To the person who is weary of religion, Jesus offered the following invitation, "Come to me, all who are weary and heavy laden, and I will give you rest. Take my yoke upon you and learn from me, for I am gentle and lowly in heart, and you will find rest for your souls. For my yoke is easy and my burden is light" (Matthew 11:28-30).

My joy is full after traveling this literary journey with you, and I pray that I will see you in heaven. Until then, remember this: all of the mysteries of life are solved in Jesus Christ, including mysteries of the afterlife.

Notes

1. Charlotte Allen, "So You Want to Live Forever: Immortality Through Advanced Technology and Primitive Diet," *The Weekly Standard*, Vol. 19, No. 33, May 12, 2014.

2. Lee Dye, "Living Longer: Increasing Lifespan May Be in Our Control," accessed May 9, 2014, http://abcnews.go.com/Technology/humans-live-forever-longevity-research-suggests-longer-life/story?id=17100148.

3. Philip Yancey, "Eternity in Our Hearts," July 21, 2009, http://odb.org/2009/07/21/eternity-in-our-hearts/.

4. Saint Augustine, *Confessions* (New York: Penguin, 1961).

5. Ibid.

6. Hank Hanegraaff, "Body, Soul, and Spirit: Monism, Dichotomy, or Trichotomy?" Christian Research Institute, accessed May 15, 2014, http://www.equip.org/perspectives/body-soul-and-spirit-monism-dichotomy-or-trichotomy.

7. Ron Rhodes, *The Wonder of Heaven* (Eugene, Oregon: Harvest House, 2009), 22-23.

8. "So You Want to See Your Cartoon in *The New Yorker*?" accessed August 18, 2014, http://www.cbsnews.com/news/the-new-yorker-cartoon-editor-bob-mankoff-on-60-minutes/.

9. Erwin Lutzer, *One Minute After You Die* (Chicago: Moody, 2007), 37.

10. Ibid., p. 39.

11. John F. MacArthur, *The Glory of Heaven* (Wheaton, Illinois: Crossway, 1998), 71.

12. Rob Bell, *Love Wins* (New York: HarperOne, 2012), xiii.

13. Justo L. Gonzalez, *The Story of Christianity* (San Francisco, California: Harper Collins, 1985), 20-21.

14. "Who Is James Van Praagh?" on James Van Praagh's official website, http://www.vanpraagh.com.

15. "About Me," on Theresa Caputo's official website, http://www.theresacaputo.com.

16. J.F. Walvoord and R.B. Zuck, *The Bible Knowledge Commentary: An Exposition of the Scriptures* (Vol. 1) (Wheaton, Illinois: Victor Books, 1985), 296.

17. Caputo, "About Me."

18. Warren Wiersbe, *The Bible Exposition Commentary* (Vol. 2) (Wheaton, Illinois: Victor Books, 1996), 92.

19. Angela Johnson, "76% of Americans are living paycheck-to-paycheck," *CNN Money*, June 24, 2013, http://money.cnn.com/2013/06/24/pf/emergency-savings/index.html.

20. Haddon Robinson, *What Jesus Says About Successful Living* (Grand Rapids, Michigan: Discovery House Publishing, 1989), 212.

21. Warren Wiersbe, *The Bible Exposition Commentary* (Vol. 1) (Wheaton, Illinois: Victor Books, 1996), 211.

22. Rhodes, 101.

23. Ibid., 121.

24. Phillip Johnson, "The Burpo-Malarkey Doctrine," accessed September 29, 2014, http://www.gty.org/blog/B121018/the-burpomalarkey-doctrine.
25. Betty Eadie, *Embraced by the Light* (New York: Gold Leaf Press, 1992).
26. Johnson, "The Burpo-Malarkey Doctrine."
27. Ibid.
28. Robert Jeffress, *How Can I Know?* (Franklin, Tennessee: Worthy Publishing, 2012), 130.
29. Ibid, 131.
30. Johnson, "The Burpo-Malarkey Doctrine."
31. Ron Charles, "'The Boy Who Came Back from Heaven' actually didn't, books recalled," *The Washington Post* online, January 16, 2015, accessed February 10, 2015, http://www.washingtonpost.com/blogs/style-blog/wp/2015/01/15/boy-who-came-back-from-heaven-going-back-to-publisher/.
32. Wiersbe, *The Bible Exposition Commentary* (Vol. 2), 464.
33. Jeffress, 150.
34. J. Oswald Sanders, *Heaven: Better By Far* (Grand Rapids, Michigan: Discovery House, 1993), 91.
35. Bodie Hodge, "How Long Was the Original Cubit?" *Answers*, March 19, 2007, accessed October 13, 2014, https://answersingenesis.org/noahs-ark/how-long-was-the-original-cubit/.
36. Rhodes, 122.
37. W.A. Criswell and Paige Patterson, *Heaven* (Wheaton, Illinois: Tyndale House Publishers, 1991), 13.
38. C.S. Lewis, *The Weight of Glory* (San Francisco, California: HarperOne, 2001), 72.
39. Ibid., p. 76.
40. "Healing Leaves," *Answers*, July 22, 2013, accessed October 16, 2014, https://answersingenesis.org/education/spurgeon-sermons/1224-healing-leaves/.
41. John D. Morris, ""Will We Have Any Work to Do in Heaven?"" Institute for Creation Research, accessed October 15, 2014, http://www.icr.org/article/will-we-have-any-work-do-heaven/.
42. "Back from the Dead: Resuscitation Expert Says End Is Reversible," *Spiegel* Online, July 29, 2013, accessed October 16, 2013, http://www.spiegel.de/international/world/doctor-sam-parnia-believes-resurrection-is-a-medical-possibility-a-913075.html.
43. John Walvoord, *End Times: Understanding Today's World Events in Bible Prophecy* (Nashville, Tennessee: Word Publishing, 1998), 157.
44. Henry Morris, *The Remarkable Journey of Jonah* (Green Forest, Arkansas: Master Books, 2003), 7.
45. "Taking Flight with The Birdmen: *60 Minutes* Travels to Norway to Witness One of the World's Most Extreme Sports," October 11, 2009, accessed December 22, 2014, http://www.cbsnews.com/news/taking-flight-with-the-birdmen-09-10-2009/.
46. *The Dark Knight Rises*, directed by Christopher Nolan (2012; Burbank, California: Warner Brothers, 2012), DVD.
47. Tyler Mathisen, "Cremation is the hottest trend in the funeral industry," January 22, 2012, accessed December 26, 2014, http://www.nbcnews.com/business/business-news/cremation-hottest-trend-funeral-industry-f1B8068228.
48. Randy Alcorn, "What Is Your View on Cremation vs. Burial? Do You Believe a Cremated Body Can Be Resurrected?" February 15, 2010, accessed December 27, 2014, http://www.epm.org/resources/2010/Feb/15/what-your-view-cremation-vs-burial-do-you-believe-/.

49. Peter Kreeft and Ronald Tacelli, *Handbook of Christian Apologetics* (Downers Grove, Illinois: InterVarsity Press, 1994), 282.
50. Charles Darwin, *The Autobiography of Charles Darwin,* ed. Nora Darwin Barlow, with original omissions restored (New York: W.W. Norton, 1993), 87.
51. Bertrand Russell, *Why I Am Not a Christian* (New York: Touchstone Books, 1957), 17-18.
52. Douglas Groothuis, "The Doctrine of Hell," Christian Research Institute, accessed January 7, 2015, http://www.equip.org/article/the-doctrine-of-hell/#christian-books-1.
53. Albert Mohler, Jr., "Doing Away with Hell? Part 2," March 10, 2011, accessed January 9, 2015, http://www.albertmohler.com/2011/03/10/doing-away-with-hell-part-two.
54. C.S. Lewis, *Screwtape Letters* (New York: MacMillan, 1962), 69.
55. Darwin, 87.
56. Trevin Wax, "Rejoicing in the Wrath," *Christianity Today*, accessed September 20, 2015, http://www.christianitytoday.com/ct/2012/july-august/rejoicing-in-the-wrath.html.
57. Mohler, "Doing Away with Hell? Part 2."
58. Groothuis, "The Doctrine of Hell."
59. Robert Jeffress, *Outrageous Truth: Seven Absolutes You Can Still Believe* (Colorado Springs, Colorado: Waterbrook Press, 2004), 73.
60. Michael Burer, "Gehenna and tartaroso in the Net Bible," Bible.org Blogs, April 21, 2011, accessed January 21, 2015, http://blogs.bible.org/netbible/michael_h._burer/gehenna_and_tartaro%C5%8D_in_the_net_bible.
61. Jeffress, *How Can I Know,* 142-143.
62. Rhodes, 181.
63. William Barclay, *The Letter to the Romans* (Philadelphia: The Westminster Press, 1975), p. 188.
64. Norman Geisler, "Church/Last Things," *Systematic Theology*, Vol. 4 (Minneapolis, Minnesota: Bethany House, 2005), 310.
65. Rhodes, 179.
66. "Poll: Nearly 8 in 10 Americans Believes in Angels," CBSNews.com, December 23, 2011, accessed October 27, 2014, http://www.cbsnews.com/news/poll-nearly-8-in-10-americans-believe-in-angels/.
67. Gene Edward Veith, "Angels and Demons Go Pop Culture," Ligonier Ministries, accessed October 25, 2014, http://www.ligonier.org/learn/articles/angels-and-demons-go-pop-culture/.
68. Z.C. Hodges, Hebrews. In J.F. Walvoord & R.B. Zuck (Eds.), *The Bible Knowledge Commentary: An Exposition of the Scriptures* (Vol. 2) (Wheaton, Illinois: Victor Books, 1985), 781.
69. Billy Graham, *Angels: God's Secret Agents* (New York: Doubleday & Company, 1975), 3-4.
70. Ray Stedman, *Our Riches in Christ* (Grand Rapids, Michigan: Discovery House, 1998), 148.
71. Ibid., 148
72. "About," on The Guardian Angels official website, www.guardianangels.org.
73. James Montgomery Boice, *Psalms* Vol. 2 (Grand Rapids, Michigan: Baker Books, 1996), 751.
74. John MacArthur, *The Glory of Heaven* (Wheaton, Illinois: Crossway Books, 1996), 151-152.
75. Herbert Lockyer, *All the Angels in the Bible* (Peabody, Massachusetts: Hendrickson Publishers, 1968), 9.

76. Lockyer, 9.
77. R. Albert Mohler, Jr. and Daniel Akin, "Why We Believe Children Who Die Go to Heaven," Between the Times, October 2, 2012, accessed May 29, 2015, http://betweenthetimes.com/index.php/2012/10/02/why-we-believe-children-who-die-go-to-heaven-3/.
78. Robert Lightner, *Heaven for Those Who Can't Believe* (Arlington Heights, Illinois: Regular Baptist Press, 1977), 25.
79. Ibid., 27.
80. Ibid., 44.
81. Mohler and Akin, "Why We Believe Children Who Die Go to Heaven."

About Ron Jones

Ron Jones is the lead pastor of Atlantic Shores Baptist Church in Virginia Beach and radio Bible teacher on the nationally syndicated broadcast *Something Good with Dr. Ron Jones*. A lifelong learner, Ron earned degrees from Purdue University, Dallas Theological Seminary, and the Southern Baptist Theological Seminary. He lives in Virginia with his wife, Cathryn, and their two children.

www.somethinggoodradio.org